Studies of the Northern Campus Martius In Ancient Rome

ROBERT E. A. PALMER

THE AMERICAN PHILOSOPHICAL SOCIETY

Independence Square, Philadelphia

Library of Congress Catalog Card No.: 90-55217
International Standard Book No.: 0-87169-802-1
US ISSN 0065-9746

CONTENTS

ABBREVIATED REFERENCES
(Other than Classical Authors and Their Works)

AE	*L'Année épigraphique*
Bull. Comm.	*Bulletino della Commissione Archeologica Comunale in Roma*
CAR	Ministero della Pubblica Istruzione, Direzione Generale delle Antichità e Belle Arti. *Carta Archeologica di Roma.* Tavola I-III, Florence, 1962-1977
CIL	Th. Mommsen *et al.*, *Corpus Inscriptionum Latinarum*, 16 v. Berlin, 1863-
CLE	F. Buecheler *et al.*, *Carmina Latina Epigraphica*, Leipzig, 1895-
IGRRP	R. Cagnat, *Inscriptiones Graecae ad Res Romanas Pertinentes*, 4 v., Paris, 1911-1927
IGUR	L. Moretti, *Inscriptiones Graecae Urbis Romae.* Rome, 1968-
ILS	H. Dessau, *Inscriptiones Latinae Selectae*, 3 v., Berlin, 1892-1906
LCL	Loeb Classical Library of the Harvard University Press
MAAR	*Memoirs of the American Academy in Rome*
NdSc	Accademia Nazionale dei Lincei, *Notizie degli scavi di Antichità*
OGIS	W. Dittenberger, *Orientis Graeci Inscriptiones Selectae*, 2 v., Leipzig, 1903-1905
PIR²	E. Groag *et al.*, *Prosopographia Imperii Romani*, 2nd ed.
PLRE	A. H. M. Jones *et al.*, *Prosopography of the Later Roman Empire*, vols. 1 and 2, Cambridge, 1971-1980
RE	A. Pauly *et al.*, *Real-Encyclopädie der classischen Altertumswissenschaft*, Stuttgart, 1893-
TLL	*Thesaurus Linguae Latinae*, Munich, in progress

PREFACE

Both sections of this monograph treat ancient sites and monuments in the northern Campus Martius. For centuries during the republic the field of the god Mars lay outside the city of Rome on its northwestern limit. Some political activities (for example, public assemblies of citizens) and many religious activities (for example, the cult of Mars) took place there. Although some temples were erected immediately outside the city, we have little reason to suppose that the field was home to inhabitants. Housing, markets and necessary services are attested only in the waning days of republican government.

Pompey and Caesar began to alter the aspect of the land with a theater and its great colonnade, a hall of assembly and on the very edge of the city a new forum with a temple. Before the beginning of the Christian era the emperor Augustus and his son-in-law Agrippa quickened the process of urbanization with a building program. None of the changes worked between 55 and 12 B.C. could have been made without the government's repeated attempts, begun in 54 B.C., to bring the Tiber River under control so that the field ceased to suffer periodic flooding. Total security from inundation proved a fool's errand, but such success attended these ancient efforts that the Campus Martius was destined to be the heart of medieval Rome.

Both of the following parts of this monograph contain some discussion of Roman neighborhood organization, a subject on which the author is preparing a book. But, for the most part, this essay is addressed to problems of a broader scope. The first section grew entirely out of a need to explain the name of one of the Roman neighborhoods. Although advances in our knowledge can be claimed, the topographical preciseness we would like could not be gained. The second and longer section, on the other hand, is devoted only in part to a document of a Roman neighborhood. Within a broad, circumscribed area adjacent to the Tiber River several discoveries from the earth permit a re-examination of the use of the land with topographical detail.

The entire study may stand as a story of the development of the terrain from the end of the republic to the onset of church building.[1]

---

[1]The author wishes to acknowledge with thanks help, especially for the first section, received from R. Bates, R. Brilliant, the late L. W. Daly, E. R. Knauer, G. N. Knauer, and S. Panciera.

PART I. INTRODUCTION

In 61 B.C. Cn. Pompeius returned from two consecutive victories to celebrate a triumph on two consecutive days. Sometime during his recent campaigns Pompey had vowed a temple to Minerva. At his return he paid his vow but seems to have left no sign of this temple to Minerva on the land. A dedication roughly dated to the reign of the emperor Claudius was reared by the officers of a Roman neighborhood named the *Vicus Minervii* in Region VII. Normally this *vicus* has been wrongly charted on maps of Rome. Since Augustan Region VII has been more or less continuously occupied in modern times, few, even adventitious, discoveries in the quarter have shed any light on what stood therein from the era of building in the Campus Martius begun by the same Pompey the Great. In the following discussion the vow to Minerva, the temple that resulted, and the Neighborhood of Minerva's Precinct will be treated. Although a precise locality of the Pompeian temple and thus, in the ensuing argument, also of the neighborhood cannot be established, the re-examination of available evidence suggests that they were one and the same.

From beginning to end the career of Cn. Pompeius, Pompey the Great, exhibits anomalies in regard to the niceties of the Roman constitution and to customs of the Roman nobility. When L. Cornelius Sulla returned from the East bringing civil war to Italy, Pompey raised on private initiative a considerable armed force in Sulla's support, although he was only 23 years of age. Holding irregular commands under Sulla as dictator he persecuted the civil war in Italy and its remnants in Sicily and Africa. Upon his return in 79 from Africa he was accorded what was to be the first of three triumphs. Pompey had not held an elective office and consequently had no normal grounds for riding in triumph. The same circumstance prevailed on 29 December 71 when he triumphed again, this time for victories in civil war in the Spanish provinces. On the morrow of the second triumph he entered upon his first elective magistracy, the consulship. Normally the consulship was a noble's last elective magistracy and was held when he was 43 years old or even older. In 70 Pompey turned 36.

In 67 the popular assembly voted Pompey a command of war against pirates throughout the Mediterranean which had no parallel. To this unprecedented command was added yet another in 66 B.C. against Mithradates of Pontus whose long history of hostilities against the Romans Pompey was destined to finish in a war that engulfed the better part of the Near East.

1

I.1 The Great Pompey and Minerva

All the world knew and knows still that Gnaeus Pompeius was hailed
the Great in recognition, by his soldiers, of his similarity to king Alexander, son of Philip. The acclamation occurred first in Africa after his
defeat of Roman enemies in civil war during the brief campaign of 81
B.C. that also led to his being hailed *imperator.* The dictator Sulla himself later affirmed the surname Magnus. Presumably the ancient reports of subsequent occasions of the same acclamation testify to its
repetition, ever in conscious remembrance of the renowned Macedonian conqueror of the Persian Empire.[1]

Upon his return to Rome Pompey triumphed for a third time on 28
and 29 September 61, the latter day being his forty-fifth birthday. Now
he might boast that he had fought and conquered on three continents.
In defeating the pirates, in overthrowing Mithradates VI Eupator and
Tigranes, and in annexing the virtually anarchic remnants of the Se-
leucid empire, Pompey could make excellent political capital by his explicit boast of having made the Roman empire coincidental with the
civilized world and of rendering Asia, Rome's easternmost province
until his victories, the center of that empire whose revenues were much
enhanced. Peculiar to these victories and to their consequent triumph
in 61 are the several ancient quotations of inscriptions and placards, the
descriptions of the triumphal details, and awards to the gods by Cn.
Pompeius Magnus, again so hailed in 61 B.C. Whether solely in virtue
of an account rendered by Terentius Varro or also thanks to other contemporary sources that quoted Pompey's records immediately and di-

---

[1]At the outset Pompey's youth doubtless lent itself to the accolade recorded by Pliny *NH*
7.96 (the best evidence), Sall. *Hist.* 3.88M., Livy *Per.* 103, Dio Cassius 37.21-23, App.
Mithr. 118 (cf. 121), Plut. *Pomp.* 13. Pompey's triumphal *aureus*, with the inscriptions
'Magnus' and 'Procos', is assigned to his triumph over Spain in 71 although its obverse
bears the image of "Africa"; see Crawford (below, n. 30) no. 402. For visible proof consis-
tent with the written sources on Pompey as the latter-day Alexander, see A. Heuss,
"Alexander der Grosse und die politische Ideologie des Altertums," *Antike und Abendland* 4
(1954): 81-82; D. Michel, *Alexander als Vorbild für Pompeius, Caesar und Marcus Antonius:
Archäologische Untersuchungen, Coll. Latomus* 94 (1967): 35-66; O. Weippert, *Alexander-
Imitatio und römische Politik in republikanischer Zeit,* Diss. Würzburg 1972, 56-104; P.
Green, "Caesar and Alexander: *aemulatio, imitatio, comparatio,*" *Amer. Jour. Ancient History*
3 (1978): 1-26, esp. pp. 4-5, and J. M. C. Toynbee, *Roman Historical Portraits* (London
and Ithaca 1978) 24-28. Also the general studies of Pompey, esp. that by van Ooteghem
(below, n. 2), have discussions of Pompey's impersonation. So closely linked were the
fame of Alexander and Pompey that in his extraordinary and fanciful excursus on what
Romans would have been alive to defeat Alexander had he but ventured west (9.17-19),
Livy could not keep himself from fetching the *exemplum* of Magnus Pompeius from afar
(9.17.6). Plutarch, however, declined formally to compare Alexander and Pompey. Since
we lack his comparison of the lives of Alexander and Caesar whom he paired we cannot
be sure what apology he might have adduced if any. Green, "Caesar and Alexander,"
reaches the conclusion that Caesar himself was little affected by comparisons with Alexander.

rectly, the surviving notices enrich our knowledge of a triumph which was marked especially by Pompey's gift of the *delubrum* to Minerva.[2]

Pliny's elaborate and indignant description of the gems and precious metals borne in this third triumph includes mention of a mosaic made in pearls whereon Pompey has "swept back" hair. This coiffure represents Pompey as no other than Alexander.[3] Among the costly sculptures were gold statues of Minerva, Mars, Apollo.[4] Pompey, himself, wore Alexander's very mantle. He had won it from Mithradates.[5] The Pontic overlord had doubtless exhibited such an imperial relic because he, too, pretended to be the new Alexander.[6] Accompanied in triumph by the painting of his world conquest,[7] Pompey left little room for doubt about his historical role.

What remains today unknown is the reason why Pompey the Great chose to honor Minerva to whom he had vowed a temple in the event of victory. First, what the conquering hero advertised on the temple he built and dedicated from his booty:

Cn. Pompeius Magnus imperator bello (triginta) annorum confecto, fusis fugatis occisis in deditionem acceptis hominum centiens viciens semel (oc-

---

[2]The better modern accounts of Pompey supply discussion of his achievement against the pirates and his subsequent extraordinary command against Mithradates. For example, see the following pages that give attention just to this third triumph: J. van Ooteghem, S.J., *Pompée le Grand, bâtisseur d'empire*, Acad. Roy. Belg., Mém. Cl. Lett. Sci. Mor. et Pol., 2nd ser., 49 (1954): 278-289; M. Gelzer, *Pompeius*, 2nd ed. (Munich 1959) 122-126; R. Seager, *Pompey, a political biography*, (Oxford 1979) 77-79; O. Weippert (above, n. 1) 83-86. The sources of greater importance are: Pliny *NH* 7.95-99 (*omnes tituli*, inscription on the temple of Minerva, the *praefatio* of the summary of his oriental conquests), 37.11-20 (*verba ex ipsis Pompei triumphorum actis*), and *NH* 33.151, 35.132, 36.41; Diod. Sic. 40.3.4 (an excerpt), inscription of his deeds in Asia with the dedication of votives to the "goddess"; App. *Mithr.* 116-118 (cf. 121), inscription of achievements, list of annexed territories, and the like; Plut. *Pomp.* 45-46, the same details of conquests drawn from the source of Pliny *NH* 7.95-99; Dio Cass. 37.21 reports the explicit claim to have conquered the *oikoumene* through a legend on a painting carried on one of the triumphal floats; also see Florus 1.40.31. Weippert (above, n. 1) 92-94, rightly follows Münzer's identification of Pliny's source as M. Terentius Varro, but it should be noted that Pliny emphasizes direct quotation of Pompey's record, and in his first book Pliny lists as one of his Latin sources *acta*. At *NH* 7.99 Pliny also seems to know a speech Pompey delivered at a public meeting. Aside from minor discrepancies Pliny, Diodorus and Plutarch convey much the same burden of Pompey's extravagant claims. Seager, p. 27, affirms what Gelzer, p. 123, offered as an alternative conjecture that the "goddess" in the excerpt from Diodorus was Venus Victrix, recipient of a temple in Pompey's theater almost a decade later. That is most improbable. For the narrow confines of the shrines to Venus Victrix and other deities in the theater see L. Richardson, Jr., "A note on the architecture of the *Theatrum Pompeii* in Rome," Amer. Jour. Arch. 91 (1987): 123-126.

[3]Pliny *NH* 37.11-20. This detailed discussion of Pompey's third triumph embraces mostly the extravagant items on display and omits the routine pieces and persons. See Michel, Weippert and Toynbee (above, n. 1).

[4]Pliny, ibid.; cf. 33.151.

[5]App. *Mithr.* 117.

[6]See, e.g., Toynbee (above, n. 1) 115-116.

[7]Dio Cass. 37.21.2. Pompey's claim to world conquest was acknowledged at Miletopolis when he was styled as "warden of land and sea" (*ILS* 9459) and nearly a century later acknowledged anew as triumphing over the world (Manil. *Astr.* 1.793-794).

taginta tribus), depressis aut captis navibus (octingentis sex et quadraginta), oppidis castellis (mille quingentis octo et triginta) in fidem receptis, terris a Maeotis ad Rubrum mare subactis, votum merito Minervae. hoc est breviarium eius ab oriente.

Then follows a quotation of a *praefatio*.[8] Diodorus directly quoted a different inscription whose content approximates the two quotations in Pliny. Today this excerpt closes, ". . . he, by confiscation of the statues and the images set up to the gods, as well as other valuables taken from the enemy, has dedicated to the goddess twelve thousand and sixty pieces of gold and three hundred and seven talents of silver."[9]

No source tells us when or why he made the vow to Minerva or where he built the vowed temple, or what it held. Moreover, no temple or shrine of Minerva known to have stood in Rome has been related to this votive temple whose locality has thus remained totally unknown.

Perhaps we shall remain forever without knowledge of where Pompey the Great was when he made his vow. On the other hand, we can gain an adequate idea of why he vowed to Minerva, a goddess to whom Roman generals had paid scant prior attention. The key is to be found in the story of Alexander the Great.

In 334 Alexander, not yet so great, came to Ilium. As the descendant of Achilles, he sacrificed to Athena in her old temple, a temple he later intended to rebuild. He carried away a sacred shield.[10] In the same year he sent captured Persian panoplies to Athena of Athens in thanks for his victory at the Granicus.[11] At the turn of the year Alexander found himself at Soloi in Cilicia where he sacrificed and gave "votive" games, *vota pro salute,* to Asclepius of Soloi and to Athena of Magarsos, Soloi's neighbor, because he had recovered from an illness.[12] After the battle of the Issus in 333 Alexander set up on the bank of the Pinarus River altars to Zeus, to Heracles and to Athena.[13] The pattern emerges clearly with the subsequent notice that before the battle of Gaugamela (Arbela) Alexander made sacrifice to king Zeus and Athena Nikaia.[14]

---

[8]Pliny *NH* 7.97-98. Plut. *Pomp.* 45 gives a like list of men, towns, forts and ships taken or destroyed. The *praefatio triumphi* perhaps belongs to a senate decree.

[9]Diod. Sic. 40.4, here quoted in the *LCL* translation. For the priceless articles see *NH* 33.14, 37.11ff., where it is also said that he donated tableware of agate to Capitoline Jupiter at this triumph of 61 B.C. Strabo 12.3.31 (C 556) reports that the best of Mithradates' treasure was dedicated by Pompey on the Capitol. Although it would have been unusual, Pompey might have bestowed gifts upon the Minerva of the Capitoline triad as well as on Jupiter. For the idols of barbarian divinities see App. *Mithr.* 117.

[10]Arr. *Anab.* 1.11.7ff., Diod. Sic. 17.17.5-18.1, 18.4.5, Strabo 13.1.26-27 (C 593-595), Plut. *Alex.* 15.4. See H. U. Instinsky, *Alexander der Grosse am Hellespont* (Godesberg 1949) 54-60.

[11]Arr. *Anab.* 1.16.7, quoting an inscription.

[12]Arr. *Anab.* 2.5.8-9, Curt. Ruf. 3.7.3; also see Paus. 8.28.1 for Alexander and Asclepius elsewhere.

[13]Curt. Ruf. 3.12.27; cf. Arr. *Anab.* 1.11.7 who would tentatively set this act at his very arrival in Asia.

[14]Curt. Ruf. 4.13.15: Rex Iuppiter, Minerva Victoria. I have taken Minerva Victoria to be one goddess with the epithet Victoria but two goddesses, Athena and Nike, may have

Early in 327 Alexander sacrificed to Athena and Nike,[15] and later in
the same year he apparently planted altars to Minerva and to Nike on
the Rock of Mt. Aornus and proceeded to the Cophen River by way of
Nicaea where he also sacrificed to Athena.[16] Finally, at the fortress of
the Malli in India the wounded and imperiled Alexander was protected
and saved by the same sacred shield he had lifted eight years earlier
from the temple of Athena Ilias.[17]

The descendant of Achilles enjoyed the same divine protection as had
been accorded his heroic ancestor. No divinity figures so prominently
as Athena in the Alexander history. Not surprising in these terms,
therefore, is Pompey's vow to Minerva when confronting Mithradates,
an enemy so well matched as to impersonate the same legendary king
of Macedon. But we cannot be sure that Pompey had not earlier vowed
his shrine to Minerva/Athena in the war with the pirates. His achievements in the pirate war are also mentioned in the documents of the
Asian campaign cited in Pliny, Diodorus, Appian and Plutarch.[18]

On his way to his new command against the pirates, Pompey, though
in a hurry, made a brief side trip to Athens to sacrifice to the gods.[19]
Doubtless, Athena figured in Pompey's prayers there. As for Ilium and
Athena Ilias there is no indication that Pompey ever visited Ilium, the
presumed successor to Troy (see n. 23), yet Roman knowledge and
veneration of Athena Ilias reached back over a century.

On the eve of his war with Rome and before crossing to Greece in 192
B.C. Antiochus III sacrificed at Ilium to Athena. Two years later the
Roman admiral Livius Salinator also sacrificed to her. Then in that
same year the consul L. Cornelius Scipio went to Ilium and sacrificed
to Athena while acknowledging to the townspeople Roman descent
from Trojans.[20] Apparently such a historical claim had been asserted
earlier by the Romans in dealing with Antiochus's predecessor ca.

been intended. That Curtius Rufus is the single source of some of these sacrifices and
offerings is immaterial. We concern ourselves with Pompey's view of Alexander.
[15]Curt. Ruf. 8.2.32.
[16]Curt. Ruf. 8.11.24, Arr. *Anab.* 4.22.6.
[17]Arr. *Anab.* 6.9.4, cf. Diod. Sic. 17.21.2.
[18]Pliny *NH* 7.98, Diod. Sic. 20.4, App. *Mithr.* 117, Plut. *Pomp.* 45-46. The historical
inspiration affecting Pompey may be traced to Rome itself. In the Colonnade of Octavia
there was a *schola* named after Augustus' sister that contained a painting of Alexander,
Philip and Minerva (Pliny *NH* 35.114); in at least one case (ibid. 34.31) we are aware of
the installation of a work of art in the Augustan colonnade which had been an adornment
in the very colonnade it supplanted. The earlier colonnade was built in the 140s by Q.
Caecilius Metellus Macedonicus whose honorific cognomen strongly suggests the first
Roman setting for the painting which then would have been known to Pompey. For the
artistic endeavors and the buildings of and near Macedonicus's colonnade, see F. Coarelli,
Pap. Brit. Sch. Rome 45 (1977): 1-23, in which he accepts two diverse dates for the colonnade. Later Pompey installed a large painting of Alexander in the colonnades by his
theater (Pliny *NH* 35.132). Pompey, in his turn, must have perpetuated the general knowledge of a relationship between Alexander and Athena (Pallas) as can be seen in the
elegiac conceit of the tombstone inscription *CIL* VI 9604 = *ILS* 7800 = *CLE* 1253.
[19]Plut. *Pomp.* 27.3.
[20]Livy 35.43.3, 37.9.7, 37.37.13.

204.[21] Accordingly, an exemption from taxation was accorded the Il-
ienses in 89 B.C. by the Roman censor L. Julius L.f. Caesar out of
veneration for Athena Ilias.[22] When Strabo gives a brief historical
sketch of Ilium and Athena Ilias, he mentions the destruction by the
mutineer Fimbria in 85 B.C. and benefactions by Sulla and Caesar but
none by Pompey.[23]

Besides Athens and Ilium whose Athena Alexander the Great honored, another town could have figured in Pompey's vow to Minerva.
The Athena at Cilician Soloi was the recipient of votive games, as was
also Asclepius, given by the Macedonian prince. Soloi had been an
important haven for the pirates and became the site of one of Pompey's
thirty-nine colonies in Greece and Asia Minor, colonies named Pompeiopolis, Nikopolis, Megalopolis, Magnopolis and Diospolis. Soloi itself was rechristened Pompeiopolis. Pompey, in the manner of
Alexander, dotted the map with settlements in remembrance of himself.[24] As the founder (oikistes) he earned divine honors.[25] In all likelihood Pompey put in an appearance at Soloi/Pompeiopolis.

Not only are the Julii Caesares on record as protectors of Ilium and
its Athena,[26] the dictator himself seems to have broadcast the "conversion" of Pompey's tutelary goddess to himself. So, he writes in his memoirs on the civil war, "likewise it is well known that at Elis in the
precinct of Minerva, by counting backward in reckoning the days from
that day when Caesar won his favorable battle, the statue of Victory,
formerly set up before Minerva herself and facing Minerva's image,
turned about toward the hinges and threshold of the shrine."[27] Only an
unbeliever could ignore the religious significance of this heaven-sent
message of the victory at Pharsalus when Caesar decisively defeated
Pompey.

---

[21]So Claudius in Suet. Claud. 25.3.
[22]ILS 8770 = OGIS 440 = IGRRP 4, no. 194 (cf. nos. 195, 197, 200). Cf. R. K. Sherk,
Roman Documents from the Greek East (Baltimore 1969) no. 53, where this evidence is not
taken into account. Strabo (next note) confuses the censor with the dictator in the first
award of this exemption. Perhaps the dictator affirmed the censorial award.
[23]Strabo 13.1.26-27 (C 593-595). On the Caesars and Ilium see above, n. 22, and S.
Weinstock, Divus Julius (Oxford 1971) 17, esp. n. 5. To be sure, Pompey was honored by
the people of Ilium (IGRRP 4, no. 198 omitting a cognomen) but one may rightly wonder
where was he not honored. The dedication shows no signs of special thanks. Compare his
unusual treatment at Mytilene, where Pompey was benefactor, savior and founder (IG-
RRP 4, nos. 49-55, 80) or on Samos (ibid. no. 1710).
[24]Strabo 8.7.5 (C 387-388) and 14.3.3 (C 665) tells us that Pompey planted ex-pirates at
Achaean Dyme and Cilician Soloi, the latter renamed Pompeiopolis, founded in 67 B.C.
(Dio Cass. 36.37.5-6). Cf. App. Mithr. 115; Plut. Pomp. 45.2 where Pompey's total number of 39 colonies is given. Dyme, too, had an apparently important cult of Athena (Paus.
7.17.9). For discussion of Pompey's colonies and evidence beyond the authors see Miltner
RE 21.2. (1952) col. 2117, van Ooteghem (above, n. 2) 248-249.
[25]See Michel (above, n. 1) 48-50. Even on Delos there was also a cult association of
Pompeiastai; see Inscr. Délos vol. 4, nos. 1651 and 1797. It was probably the consequence
of gratitude to the Great One.
[26]See Strabo (above, n. 23) and Weinstock (above, n. 23).
[27]Caes. BC 3.105.

Until his defeat at Pharsalus in 48 B.C. Pompey could have been thought to enjoy the favors of Minerva, a Minerva whom he chose to venerate as the proper object of a latter-day Alexander. His vow and its fulfillment resulted in a temple to Minerva at Rome. That his triumph in 61 was held for two days at the end of September, and one of them his forty-fifth birthday,[28] may have held the further significance that the month belonged to (Capitoline) Minerva.[29]

I.2 Minerva in Triumph

In the last decades of republican government the silver coinage, usually denarii, may indicate the divine patronage accorded to or claimed by the Romans and their generals. Since no new temple is known to have been dedicated to Minerva between the conquest of Old Falerii in 241 B.C. and Pompey's *delubrum* after 61 B.C., we are especially obliged to seek what information we can from the immediate coinage. She reappears sporadically on coins in Pompey's youth for reasons that are not clear, either from the coins themselves or from other sources.

Only in the recent past Romans had resumed the representation of Minerva on the silver coinage. She is usually shown with one or more attributes of war and victory.[30] On two coins from different moneyers she reappears in 90 B.C. after a long absence from the coinage.[31] A semis has an obverse of Apollo and Minerva in a triumphal car; three denarii have obverses of Minerva, sometimes with a Winged Victory, and a reverse of the same Minerva in a triumphal car.[32] Both these moneyers are minting not only when the Social War is at its height but during the consulship of L. Julius Caesar, who as censor in the following year or years awarded Ilium tax exemption out of veneration for Athena.[33] A few years later C. Licinius Macer again joins Apollo (obv.) and Minerva riding in triumph (rev.).[34] Indeed, thereafter Minerva is not associated with any "Pompeian" sentiment and, on the contrary, is made later to represent Caesarian and triumviral partisanship. No coin

---

[28]A. Degrassi, *Inscr. Ital.* 13.1, p. 566.

[29]Idem, *Inscr. Ital.* 13.2, p. 509.

[30]M. Crawford, *Roman Republican Coinage*, 2 vols. (Cambridge 1974) nos. 341/5, 342/4-6, 354/1, 389, 454/3, 455/6, 463/2, 465/5, 494/37-38; see p. 737.

[31]A reappearance that Weinstock (above, 23) 100-101 cannot explain, for she "takes the place" of Roma and Venus. He believes she is Parthenos on the coin of 42 B.C. If a Caesarian Athena, she ought to have been Athena of Elis.

[32]Crawford, nos. 341/5, 342/4-6. The moneyers were Q. Titius and C. Vibius C.f. Pansa. In the second case, Crawford, p. 511, believes that Minerva is portrayed because the Vibii so esteemed her. But other explanations can be adduced, and the C. Vibius Varus issuing triumviral coins (no. 494) is not a Pansa.

[33]Above, at n. 22.

[34]Crawford, no. 354/1 in 84 B.C. He is the historian. Another Licinian moneyer, a Nerva, also exhibits Minerva (454/3). They, too, are not related.

with Minerva was minted when Pompeius Magnus brokered and shared power.

The ten coins on which Minerva appears from 90 to 42 B.C. were issued by eight moneyers, four of whom coined after Pharsalus and under other than Pompeian influence. Shared characteristics can be seen at a glance:

YEAR	CRAWFORD NOS.	MONEYER	VICTORY	TRIUMPHAL CAR	APOLLO
90	341/5	Q. Titius		X	X
90	342/4-6	C. Vibius C.f. Pansa	X	X	X
84	354/1	C. Licinius L.f. Macer		X	X
76	389	L. Rustius			
47	454/3	A. Licinius Nerva	X		
46	465/5	C. Considius Paetus	X	X	
45	476	C. Clovius	X		
42	494/37-38	C. Vibius Varus	X		

Only the coin of L. Rustius seems to have been influenced by his own familial piety. Indeed the two coins of Vibius Varus, last on the list, show both Minerva and Hercules. Hercules, too, had been a patron of Pompey's, the recipient of a temple at his second triumph a decade earlier.[35] The recurrence of Minerva as goddess of victory and in connection with Hercules points to the great Caesar's victory over the great Pompey.[36]

Although the reason for a revival of Minerva on the coinage in 90 B.C. is not forthcoming, the revived Minerva is shown in the attitude of victory, whether in a triumphal car or attended by Victory herself. The coins of the Forties suggest Caesarian victory brought about by the goddess's transfer of victory from Pompey to Caesar.

It is inappropriate and unnecessary to review further the history of Minerva in Rome before Pompey. No temple of Minerva built after the third century is known before Pompey dedicated a new shrine to her in the wake of his victories in the Near East. Furthermore, no Minervian temple with a known site can be attributed to Pompey. Indeed, we are ignorant of the locality of three temples of Minerva, for two of which we know the region. The fourth century *Notitia urbis Romae* alone con-

---

[35]Pliny *NH* 7.95, which god I have associated with his Spanish victories; see R. E. A. Palmer, "C. Verres' Legacy of Charm and Love to the City of Rome: A New Document" *Pont. Accad. Rom. Arch. Rend.,* 51-52 (1978-79, 1979-80): 114-115.

[36]By this date Pompey's son Sextus Pompeius had switched to exhibiting on coins his veneration for Pietas and for Neptune (cf. Dio Cass. 48.31.5); Crawford, nos. 477, 511. For a possible interest on the part of Octavian in Minerva Medica see Dio Cass. 47.41 and Lact. *Div. Inst.* 2.7.22.

veys the information that a temple of Minerva stood in Region I ('Porta Capena'). Pompey's temple of Minerva does not have even so much as an Augustan region noted by Pliny and Diodorus. The third shrine of Minerva is never so much as listed among the goddess's properties in the city. Instead the epigraphic document that yields the record is ignored in discussions of Minerva's temples in the city and is charted on any plan of find-sites in clear defiance of internal and external evidence.

I.3 The Minervium in Region VII

A compital inscription from year 50, i.e. ca. A.D. 42,[37] was found north of the Aurelianic Wall in soil rich only in evidence of cemeteries.[38]

Statae Matri / Aug(ustae) sacrum/ mag(istri) reg(ione) VII vico Minervi, / anni L, / Ap. Arrenus Appianus, / C. Cornelius Eutychus, / Sex. Plotius Quartio, / C. Vibius Phylades. / dedicata est / (ante diem) XVII k(alendas) Sep(tembres) / lustratione.[39]

When Lanciani and Lugli-Gismondi chart this street of the Minervium they put it in Regione VI *and* both within and without the Aurelianic wall to make the find-site conformable to the testimony of the text which says the *vicus* lay in Region VII (later 'Via Lata').[40] No urban *vicus* lay outside the line of the later wall, let alone in a graveyard.[41] This stone was not and could not have been found where the four *magistri* reared it. Doubtless it was dumped in a cemetery at some later time. The confines of Region VII extended roughly north from the Capitol by the Via Flaminia (Lata) to where the later Porta Flaminia was and

---

[37]In the early years after their refoundation by Augustus the officers of a neighborhood (*vicus*) serving as priests of the crossroads shrine (*compitum*) would tacitly acknowledge the Augustan dispensation by dating with the compital era from the moment when Augustus had given statues of the neighborhood Lares. Rough dating puts most Augustan refoundations of neighborhood cults in the year 7 B.C.; see G. Gatti, "L'era dei vico-magistri" *Bull. Comm.* (1906) 198-208; and below, n. 43.

[38]*CAR* II-C 87, pp. 50-51, strangely enough we know the name of and place of the find-site from a discovery of *CIL* VI 10241 = *ILS* 7912 in the Vigna Pelucchi, namely *in monumento T. Flavi Artemidori quod est via Salaria in agro Volusi Basilides ientibus ab urbe parte sinistra*, from the era of the Antonines. Rarely have we such certain proof of a stone's later intrusion into an alien context. See Plan 1.

[39]*CIL* VI 766 = *ILS* 3309.

[40]R. Lanciani, *Forma Vrbis Romae* (Milan 1893-1907) tav. 2; Lugli-Gismondi on their wall map of 1949, followed by F. Scagnetti on his wall map of 1979.

[41]In G. Lugli's *Fontes ad topographiam veteris urbis Romae* vol. 4, book 14, "Regio VII: Via Lata," he will have changed his mind because the collaborator of this book, V. Fraticelli Massaccesi, p. 366, no. 34 writes of the Vicus Minervi in *CIL* VI 766: aetate media via Pinciana fortasse appellabatur. Cf. H. Riemann, *RE* 20.2 (1950) col. 1494. No one has admitted what must be true of this inscription that it was uprooted and moved. Where it was found was anciently called the Via Salaria (above, n. 38), and was immediately outside Region VI, not Region VII.

north from Trajan's Forum at the foot of the Quirinal to where the later Porta Pinciana was and had an E-W border on the northern limit following the later line of the wall (See Plan 1).[42] In a word the Minervium that named the neighborhood must be sought on the northeastern Campus Martius or the western slopes of Monte Pincio at that hill's western end.

There is an internal clue in the text of the inscription as to the circumstances of its occasion. Stata Mater was a divinity especially worshipped in Roman neighborhoods because of her capacity to repel fire.[43] In October of A.D. 38 and again a few years later under Claudius fires raged in the *Aemiliana,* located somewhere in adjacent Region IX. On the second occasion the fire burned so long that Claudius took up a post in the Diribitorium to assist in its extinction.[44]

I.4 Pompey's Triumphal Monuments

About Region VII rather little is known thanks to its continuous occupation for many centuries. However, there are traces of Pompey the Great in what was to be circumscribed later as Augustan Region VII. The two gazetteers of the city report in Region VII an equestrian statue or statues (*equum* or *equos*) of *Tigridates* (sic!), king of the Armenians. Topographers merely remark that this may be some sort of memorial of the visit of Tiridates to Neronian Rome and so emend the king's name.[45] I prefer, however, to read *Tigranis* and refer the monument to Pompey's triumph. Two Tigranes opposed Pompey. One, the king of the Armenians, betrayed his father-in-law Mithradates and later became Pompey's client; the other, grandson of Mithradates as well as the son of the homonymous king, was brought by Pompey to Rome and carried in his triumph.[46] The Armenians of this era were renowned horse breed-

---

[42]See the same G. Lugli, *I monumenti antichi ecc.* "Supplemento" (Rome, 1940) to vol. 3, pp. 24 and 35; Riemann (above, no. 41) col. 1509; for the older line of *continentia* observed by Aurelian in building the wall, see R. E. A. Palmer, "Customs on Market Goods Imported into the City of Rome," *MAAR* 36 (1980): 217ff.

[43]Festus 416/17L. There are three other compital dedications to Stata Mater: in 6 B.C., in year 2, and in A.D. 12 (*CIL* VI 763-765); and a compital dedication to Stata Fortuna, also in A.D. 12 (VI 761); as well as two neighborhoods named for Stata (VI 975 in Reg. XIV; 36809, in Reg. II). A compital dedication to Volcanus Quietus and Stata Mater was made in year 5 (*CIL* VI 802) and to Volcanus Quietus in year L . . . (VI 801), the neighborhood of the Minervium dedicated to Stata Mater with purification on 16 August. On 23 August fell the annual Volcanalia; see Degrassi, *Inscr. Ital.* 13.2, pp. 500-501.

[44]See *Fast. Ost.* for XI k. Nov. of A.D. 38 in A. Degrassi, *Inscr. Ital.* 13.1, pp. 191, 229, and Suet. *Claudius* 18.

[45]E.g., S. Platner and T. Ashby, *A Topographical Dictionary of Ancient Rome* (Oxford 1929) 202. See A. Nordh, *Libellus de regionibus urbis Romae,* Acta Inst. Rom. Reg. Suec. ser in 8°, 3, Lund 1949, p. 83, *"fortasse cum nomine Tigranes confusum."*

[46]See F. Geyer, *RE* 6AI (1936) cols. 970-978. For Pompey's claims of conquest of Tigranes and of the son's humiliation see Livy *Per.* 103, Pliny *NH* 7.98, App. *Mithr.* 104-105

ers and cavalrymen,[47] and any one of them should have been represented on a horse.

Other witness to the triumph of Pompeius Magnus may have been found in this region. In the middle of the sixteenth century both a small vineyard at the foot of the Pincian Hill and a house near the Column of Marcus Aurelius belonging to Ambrogio Lilio (Gigli) held ancient pieces pertinent to our interest: "a marble tablet on which almost in high relief is seated king, headless, and a man presenting a horse as if for tribute," "a young Hercules in full relief, holding the head of a horse by the mane," "a fine ancient head which is said to be of Pompey," "a marble tablet on which are sculptured the labors of Hercules."[48] That Hercules loomed large in Pompey's religious obligations is well established.[49] The other relief could have been part of booty or a representation of a surrender to Pompey. Some hazard subsists in interpreting these reported pieces. First, we must assume that these sculptures came from the seventh region of the ancient city where Lilio had some property, second, that they were indeed Pompeian monuments, and finally, that they had belonged to a triumphal complex related to Pompey's temple of Minerva. Such assumptions find support from the consideration of the location of the gardens of Pompey.

I.5 Pompey's Gardens

Whereas we may merely speculate on the existence and aspect of a triumphal monument of Pompey in Region VII, we seize firmer ground in discussing the site of Pompey's gardens in this district. No author explicitly states the location of these gardens. Purchased before his return in 61 B.C. and expensive, they bore the jesting name "gardens of Demetrius," perhaps wrongly interpreted as named for his infamous Gadarene freedman.[50] The gardens are thrice referred to as the upper gardens where Pompey could fortify himself with a bodyguard sur-

---

and 117, Dio Cass. 36.53.6, 37.6.2. One may compare the statue of the fourteen peoples set up at Pompey's theater; see Pliny *NH* 36.41 (cf. 7.34), Suet. *Nero* 46.1, Serv. Dan. on *Aen.* 8.72. One or more Pompeian documents listed by name the kings Pompey the Great had conquered (cf. Pliny *NH* 7.98, Diod. Sic. 40.4, App. *Mithr.* 117); their portraits, where appropriate, could have been used to represent a people (*gens* or *natio*) overcome by Pompey and exhibited in his colonnade. A contemporary response to Pompey's assertion of his patronship over kings and peoples is to be found in Dolabella's letter to Cicero (*ad Fam.* 9.9.2).

[47]See, e.g., Strabo 11.4.4 (C 502), 11.13.7 (C 525), 11.14.9 (C 530), 11.14.12 (C 530/31).

[48]R. Lanciani, *Storia degli scavi di Roma* vol. 3 (Rome 1902-1912) 103, 146-147; I have extracted from Lanciani's extract only what suits my purpose. See H. Riemann, 'Pincius Mons', in *RE* 20.2 (1950) col. 1539; cf. our Plan 1.

[49]See above n. 35.

[50]Plut. *Pomp.* 40.5, a garbled account, that apparently confirms a purchase date in the mid-60s.

rounding his villa.[51] Upper (and lower) gardens could have belonged to the slope of a hill, even the Janiculum across the Tiber. But in 61, we learn, Pompey was in his gardens outside the city awaiting his triumph and there bestowed bribes on the voters.[52] Respecting the convenience of the voters who would have been casting their ballots in the Campus Martius, this report can mean only the gardens at the *collis hortulorum*, Monte Pincio, partly in Region VII. Mark Anthony was the subsequent owner of this property.[53]

It is next attested in the hands of the Statilii, descendants of one of Augustus's generals. In the great Statilii cemetery we find record of the slave Eros *i(n)sularius ex horteis Pompeia(nis)*.[54] The salient information from the epigraphic find in the columbarium is the job of the slave from the Pompeian Gardens. An *insularius* kept an apartment house.[55] Some part of Pompey's Gardens was evidently devoted to profitable construction in succeeding generations. The several owners of these men were themselves rentiers who remained in possession until after A.D. 68. Statilia Messallina, Nero's widow, is on record as owner of four defunct tenants of this columbarium.[56] The sum of the evidence so far addressed yields the following. Pompey's Upper and Lower Gardens lay on and below the Pincian Hill. They passed from Pompey's to Anthony's ownership, and thence into the possession of the Statilii Tauri. The lower gardens, at least in part, joined the urbanized landscape of Mars's Field and held an apartment house belonging to the Statilii. Further, I suggest that in or beside the lower gardens at the foot of the Pincian Hill Pompey had built his temple to Minerva whose precinct named the *vicus* in Augustan Region VII and built a victory monument that exhibited the statue of a mounted Tigranes. (See Plan 1.)

---

[51]Ascon. pp. 36, 50, 51-52 Clark; the date is the time of Milo's trial in 52 B.C.

[52]Plut. *Pomp.* 44.3-5; Pompey was seeking the election of Afranius to the consulship. The use of *villa* (not *domus*) by Asconius (note 51) to describe his house in the gardens and the fact that Pompey could not enter the city proper before his triumph precludes any identification of the place of Pompey's sojourn with his mansion in the Carinae which lay in the middle of Rome where no building could be called *villa*.

[53]Cic. *Phil.* 2.67-68, 109; App. *BC* 3.14.49-50; Vell. Pat. 2.60.3. See Riemann (above, n. 48) cols. 1512-1513. It is the older view that Pompey's garden lay on or by the Pincian Hill; see Platner-Ashby, *TDAR*, p. 270; F. Castagnoli, "Il Campo Marzio nell'antichità," *Acc. Lincei Mem. Cl. Sc. Mor. Stor. Fil.*, ser. 8, vol. 1 (1948) pp. 144; and Lugli, *Fontes etc.* (above, n. 41) pp. 396-398. *Contra*, E. La Rocca, *La riva a mezzaluna* (Rome 1984) p. 96, n. 39, following some recent writers who would place his lower gardens at Pompey's new house by his theaters; V. Jolivet, "Les jardins de Pompée: nouvelles hypothèses." *Mel. Ecole Franç. Rome* 95 (1983): 115-138. No authority suggests that Pompey's gardens lay in the Campus Martius in the vicinity of his theater.

[54]*CIL* VI 6299; also the same Eros is found in 6215, 6217, as an officer of the burial society that possessed the columbarium.

[55]Besides the *insularius* Eros (*CIL* VI 6299) there are four other *insularii* buried there (6215, 6296-6298). None is recorded as assigned to "gardens."

[56]*CIL* VI 6596, 6619, 6620, 6625. Not once is Nero given the title *Aug.* because, we must assume, he is dead. Earlier than her marriage to Nero she was *Tauri f.* (see *CIL* VI 9191, 9842).

I.6 Conclusion

The location of Pompey's temple of Minerva built after 61 B.C. cannot be made precise. Indirect evidence of his triumphal monuments in what was later Augustan Region VII of the extended city does not yield information of the exact situation. Even the case of the Minervium lying in Region VII in the reign of Claudius is bereft of topographical detail because its single document was not found in its original place. Inference from the use of the term "upper gardens" and from their proximity necessary to bribing voters causes us to situate the great man's gardens on and below the Pincian Hill. Presumably the lower gardens (never so designated) lost their horticulture to urban buildings. But this development of the terrain could have happened over a period of 125 years after Pompey's third triumph.

In the Sixties Pompey the Great vowed a temple to Minerva because he had taken Alexander the Great as his model. The Macedonian king's model was his ancestor, Homer's Achilles. Time and again Alexander accorded Athena worship. What is more, her "Trojan" shield had saved Alexander's life. Pompey's emulation of Alexander neither started nor ended in the campaigns leading to his triumph in 61 B.C. His vow to Minerva, however, represents his one known act of adherence to Alexander's religious preference.

Long years after Pompey's dedication of a temple to Minerva, the officers of a neighborhood called after a precinct of Minerva recorded their dedication to a goddess of peculiar power for Roman neighborhoods. Their inscription made in the reign of Claudius has heretofore been wrongly thought to have been found in its original place. Moreover, the evidence of the Minervium has been left out of discussion of the temples of Minerva in Rome.

Among the Roman temples of Minerva without a history the Minervium in Augustan Region VII can be identified with Pompey's temple because he presumably owned gardens in this sector and a part of these gardens underwent urbanization. From two disparate and niggardly sources are inferred triumphal monuments of Pompey lying in the same region. From the fourth-century gazetteers comes notice of an equestrian statue (or statues), now interpreted as representing Pompey's whilom enemy Tigranes, king of the Armenians and ally of Mithradates. From a less certain source comes information on some sculptures that in early modern times were housed in this sector and were then interpreted in such a way as to permit a relation to Pompey and to his earlier devotion to Hercules.

The sum of all indications suggest that we should seek Pompey the Great's temple for Minerva in Region VII at the foot of the Pincian Hill.

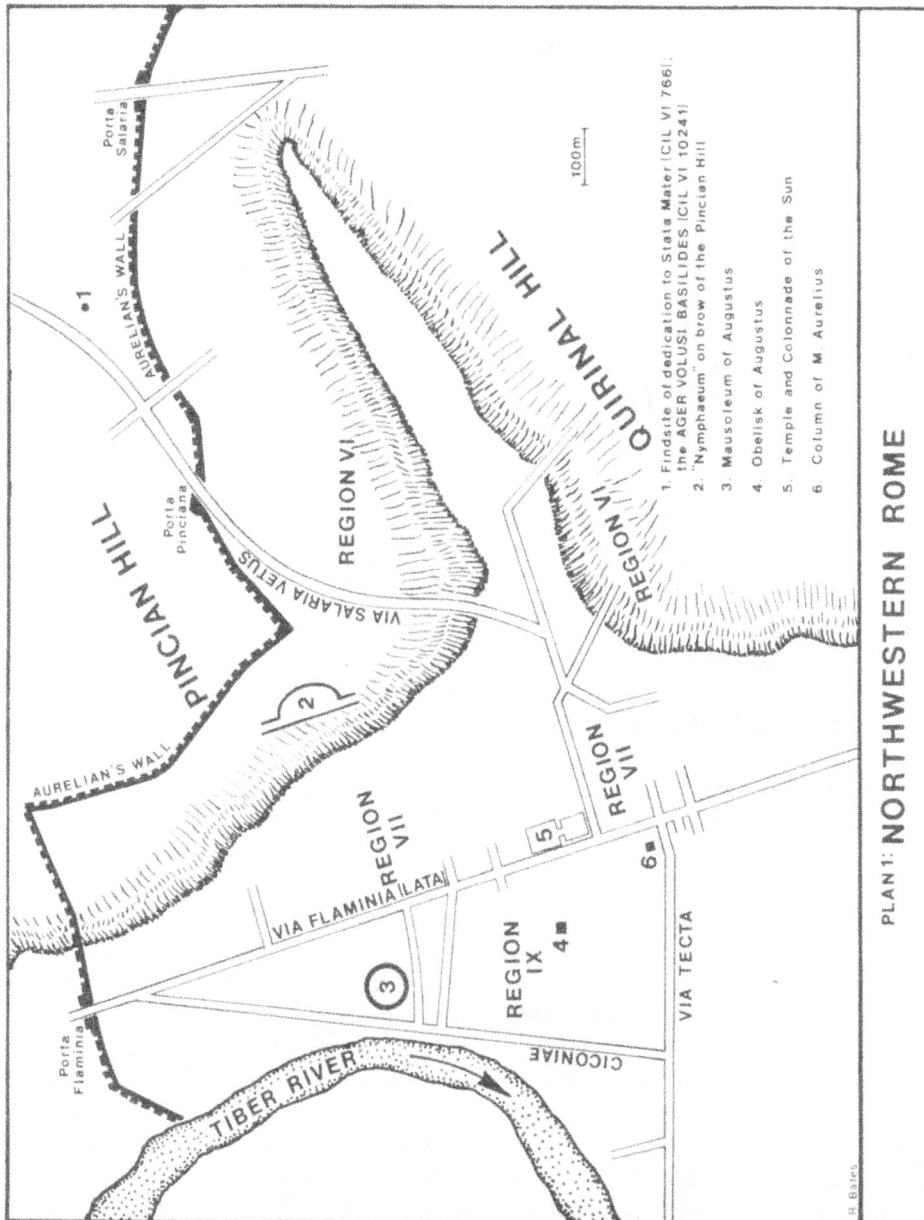

1. Findsite of dedication to Stata Mater (CIL VI 766), the AGER VOLUSI BASILIDES (CIL VI 10241)
2. "Nymphaeum" on brow of the Pincian Hill
3. Mausoleum of Augustus
4. Obelisk of Augustus
5. Temple and Colonnade of the Sun
6. Column of M. Aurelius

PLAN 1: NORTHWESTERN ROME

PLAN 2

THE NORTHERN CAMPUS MARTIUS

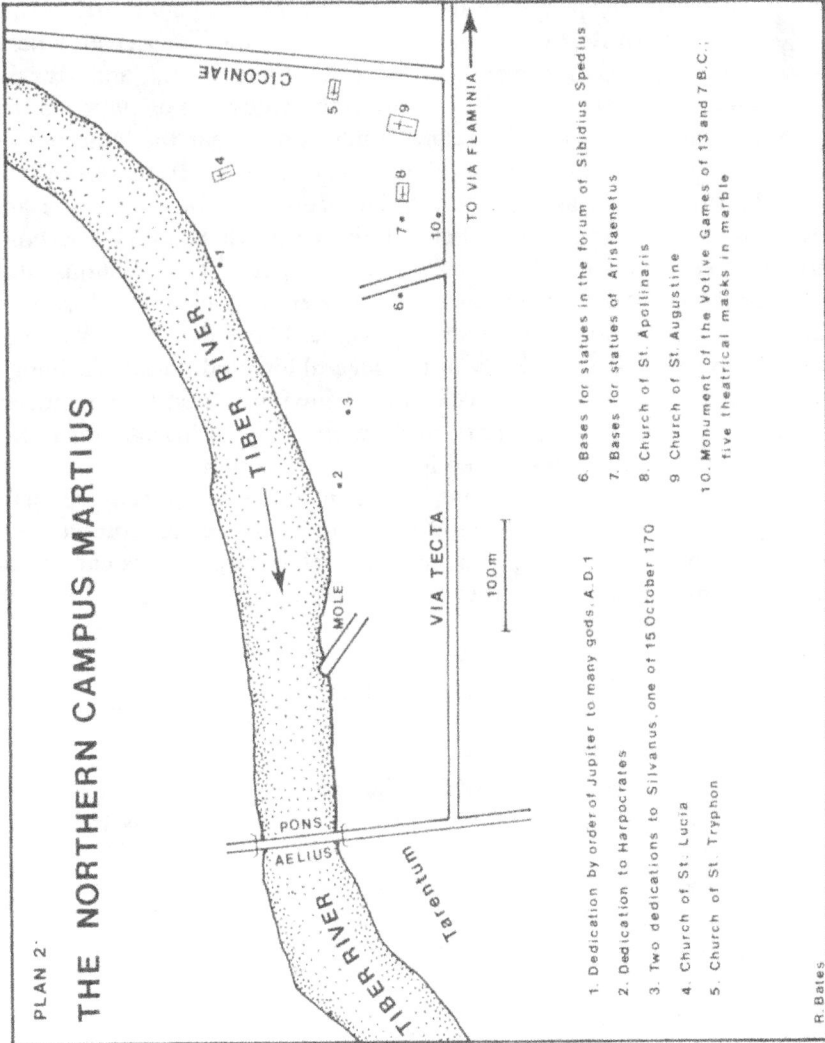

TIBER RIVER

TIBER RIVER

TIBER RIVER

CICONIAE

MOLE

PONS
AELIUS

Tarentum

VIA TECTA

100m

TO VIA FLAMINIA

1. Dedication by order of Jupiter to many gods. A.D. 1

2. Dedication to Harpocrates

3. Two dedications to Silvanus, one of 15 October 170

4. Church of St. Lucia

5. Church of St. Tryphon

6. Bases for statues in the forum of Sibidius Spedius

7. Bases for statues of Aristaenetus

8. Church of St. Apollinaris

9. Church of St. Augustine

10. Monument of the Votive Games of 13 and 7 B.C.;
    five theatrical masks in marble

R. Bates

PART II. INTRODUCTION

The following pages are devoted to the tract of land at the northern end of Roman Campus Martius near the Tiber river, where today the Lungoteveri degli Altoviti, Tor di Nona, and Marzio follow along the river. More particularly, the study has as its focus the epigraphic and epigraphically related finds in and near the churches of St. Augustine, St. Apollinaris, and St. Lucia (see Plan 2). However, in a way, the study also has a peculiar reference to the Tarentum, the ancient place at the great elbow bend in the river where every one hundred or one hundred and ten years elaborate games and religious rites were observed near the temporarily uncovered altar of the lord and lady of the Underworld. In so far as possible, I have developed an argument following the chronology of the several bits and pieces. Although the Tarentum was known as a religious shrine for at least four centuries before Augustus, the study starts with monuments of his age, for in his reign the whole sector witnessed its full urbanization.

Emphasis is placed on religious documents, whether pagan or Christian, but such an emphasis should not be mistaken for an emphasis on religion so much as an emphasis on what religious practices can tell of the changing aspect of the city.

II.1 Votive Games for Augustus' Return

The emperor Augustus himself singled out for mention two occasions when the Senate's concern for his safe return to Rome was translated into the founding of altars.[1] In 19 B.C. an altar to Fortuna Redux was voted for his return from the overseas provinces, was founded on 12 October presumably in that year, and later dedicated on 15 December. The first of these days became that of the annual celebration of the festival Augustalia.[2] In 13 B.C. an altar to Pax Augusta was voted for his return from Spain and Gaul, was founded on 4 July in that year and was dedicated on 30 January 9 B.C.[3] This justly renowned Altar of Peace was not the only senatorial acknowledgment of the prince's safe return in 13 B.C.

---

[1] Aug. *Res Gestae 11-12.*

[2] Aug. *RG* 11; A. Degrassi, *Fasti anni Numani et Iuliani, Inscriptiones Italiae* 13.2 (Rome 1963) 519-520, 538; Dio Cass. 54.10.3.

[3] Aug. *RG* 12; Degrassi, *Fasti anni Numani,* 476, 404-405; Dio Cass. 54.25.3.

Less known because Augustus did not remark them in his *Achievements* are three occasions on which votive games were decreed by the
Senate for his return. The first fell also in 13, the second in 8 and the
third, the following year 7 B.C. These three series of votive games are
recorded by inscriptions set up by the consul in charge of them and have
left virtually like texts. From each of the three texts we learn that a
consul in company with his consular colleague gave votive games to
Jupiter Optimus Maximus for the return of Augustus in accordance
with a Senate decree.

In 13 B.C., the year of the decree of the Altar of Peace, Dio reports
that Augustus was returning from the Spains, Gauls and Germanies,
that he declined the vote of an altar and entered the city by stealth at
night and that his stepson Tiberius as consul gave the votive games for
his return.[4] Augustus, as we saw, made no mention of a return from
Germany and surely accepted the voted Altar of Peace. Furthermore,
the inscription commemorating the votive games says that Tiberius's
consular colleague presided.[5] In 10 and 9 B.C. Augustus was in the
province of Gallia Lugdunensis and returned to, but did not enter,
Rome on account of the death of Drusus whom he eulogized in the
Circus Flaminius.[6] Only in the following year, 8 B.C., did he "make his
formal return," when also the consuls are said to have kept the normal
observances and included gladiatorial combats of recent captives—
presumably a mode of funeral ceremony for Drusus.[7] The votive games
for Augustus's formal return were formally held by the consul of 8 B.C.
with his colleague.[8] On the third occasion of these votive games for his
return in 7 B.C. we have no idea when Augustus actually came back to
Rome. Rather, Dio tells us that the consul Tiberius was suddenly called
away by events in Germany and left Gaius, Augustus's grandson, to
preside with his (Tiberius's) colleague. The commemorative inscription
makes Tiberius the presiding consul.[9]

Bearing in mind that the votive games were held for Jupiter Optimus
Maximus whose temple stood on the Capitol, we turn to the prove-
niences of these texts. The inscriptions for the games of the years 13
and 7 B.C. were found together in the Piazza S. Apollinare, along with
five monumental theatrical masks carved in marble.[10] (See Plan 2, no.

---

[4]Dio Cass. 54.25, 27.1 Augustus may have had reason to believe that spontaneous
exaltation would occur if he openly entered the City in daylight. An ode of Horace
written earlier (*Carm*.4.5) had expressed sentiments of longing for the return of the absent
prince; see E. Fraenkel, *Horace* (Oxford, 1957) 440-449.

[5]Aug. *RG* 12; *CIL* VI 386 = *ILS* 88.

[6]Dio Cass. 54.36.4, 55.2.2.

[7]Dio Cass 55.5.1-2. On the character of *ludi votivi* see below, nn. 10, 12.

[8]*CIL* VI 36789 = *ILS* 8894.

[9]Dio Cass. 55.8.3; *CIL* VI 385 = *ILS* 95, the best preserved of the three inscribed
records save for the excision of the name of Tiberius's fellow consul, Cn. Calpurnius
Piso.

[10]R. Lanciani, *Storia degli Scavi di Roma* vol. 2 (Rome, 1902-1912), 230 for the year
1547; *CAR* I-I, 130, p. 121. The *ludi votivi* should be reckoned as adhering to the model of

10.) The character of the monument to which such masks would have belonged and the two records of votive games suggest that the very site of the discovery was the ancient site of the games in 13 and 7 B.C. The third record, the inscription of 8 B.C., has no certain provenience. Both of its editors give warning because it was bought on the antiquarian market and was said to have come from "private property" near the Colosseum.[11]

Granted that this inscription of 8 B.C. cannot be situated precisely, we have the means to explain the apparently considerable distance between the record of 8 B.C. and the records of 13 and 7 B.C. The provenience of the latter lies close to the Tiber whose floodwaters could interrupt activity in the quarter. The three great annual ceremonies held in honor of Mars, the Equirria of 27 February, a second festival of the same name on 14 March and the October Horse of 15 October, were normally held on the Campus Martius in this sector, but in case of flood they might be held instead at the Campus Martialis on the Caelian Hill.[12] Obviously we must think of a substitute locality without regard to the later Flavian Amphitheater, to the Golden House and to the temple of the Divine Claudius[13] so that we may imagine that the ancient position of the inscription of the votive games of 8 B.C. lay near the Colosseum, that is by the Caelian Hill, because of severe flooding in that year. Indeed evidence for such circumstances, but not of an actual flood in that year, is borne out by the many inscriptions marking maintenance of the Tiber banks set up by the consuls of 8 B.C. and also by Augustus himself in 7 and 6 B.C.[14] Accordingly we are entitled to pre-

---

the Ludi Magni or Ludi Romani of September which were originally, in a sense, triumphal and at the same time the consequence of a vow (*votum* > *votivi ludi*). Capitoline Jupiter Best and Greatest was the special object of the feast day of 13 September and of all the games which grew in length to embrace 4-19 September. One of the added days had been voted to honor Augustus's deified father. Some of the games were theatrical, but most were circensian, i.e. chariot races. See Degrassi (above, n. 2) 506-507, 509. To appreciate the character of the relation between Augustus' return and Jupiter can be adduced the case of 175 or 174 B.C. when Ti. Sempronius Gracchus triumphed over the Sards (Livy 41.28.8-10; cf. A. Degrassi, *Inscr. Ital.* 13.1, p. 555): iterum triumphans in urbem Romam redit cuius rei ergo hanc tabulam donum Iovi dedit. Gracchus set up his memorial as an offering to Jupiter in the temple of Mater Matuta (Livy, *ibid.*) which marked the City entrance of the triumphal way (cf. F. Coarelli, "La Porta Trionfale e la via dei trionfi", *Dialoghi di Archeologia* 2 [1968]: 55-103). In like fashion the conqueror of Antiochus's fleet in 190 B.C. set up his dedicatory inscription for the temple of the Lares Permarini both on that temple above the doors and in the Capitoline temple of Jupiter (Livy 40.52).

[11]D. Vaglieri in *Bull. Comm.* 1903, pp. 249-251 and M. Bang at *CIL* VI 36789.

[12]See Degrassi, (above, n.2), 416, 422, 521 for the festivals; F. Castagnoli, "Il Campo Marzio nell antichità," *Acc. Naz. Lincei Mem. Sci. Mor. Stor. Fil.* ser. 8, vol. 1 (1948): 93-195, esp. 136, 140-146, for the site of these races of chariot and sacrifice of a horse.

[13]For the Campus Martialis see Ovid *Fasti* 3.519-523, Festus p. 117 L., both ultimately Augustan sources.

[14]The texts are most easily consulted in G. Lugli, *Fontes ad Topographiam veteris urbis Romae pertinentes*, 2 (Rome 1953): 72-77. The origins of the markers from 8 B.C. permit us to assume damage to the banks from north of the Porta Flaminia to over two miles south of the City; from 7/6 B.C., at the Ripetta in the north to the vicinity of the Pons

sume that the usual site of the votive games was not available in 8 B.C. because of flood waters or flood damage and that they were held somewhere near the terrain of the later Colosseum. The circumstances of the inscriptions point to the games held on the Campus Martius in 13 and 7 B.C. and on the Campus Martialis on or at the Caelian Hill in 8 B.C. In other words, the votive games for Augustus's safe return were given for Jupiter Optimus Maximus, as otherwise the annual ritual races for Mars took place.

Evidently the gladiatorial combats at what we presume to be these votive games in 8 B.C. were exceptional for the normal program.[15] The monumental marble masks more or less assure the probability that the votive games were in part theatrical and that their locality was permanently marked by some monument alluding to theatrical performances.

However that may be, the site of the votive games in 13 and 7 B.C. need not be reserved solely for such occasional games. As we shall see, other occasions arose for the stage plays and the chariot races to be produced in this sector.

II.2 Jupiter the Tragic Player

In anticipation of a more thoroughgoing reformation of the city's organization in 7 B.C. Augustus presented statues of great value to the neighborhoods (*vici*). These statues of divine patrons of the neighborhood are known to us from Suetonius and from their inscribed bases, ranging in date from 10 B.C. to A.D. 10. Suetonius cites as instances the statues of Jupiter Tragoedus and Apollo Sandaliarius.[16] Apollo Sandaliarius surely belonged to the Vicus Sandaliarius. The inscribed bases commemorate Augustus's gifts of statues, bought with New Year's offerings, to the Lares Publici, to Vulcan, to Mercury and to two others.[17] To date, the home of Jupiter the Tragic Player has remained un-

Fabricius (at the Island). In the authors the last flood to be noted had happened in 13 B.C. before Augustus returned (Dio. Cass. 53.25.2; see Suet. *Aug.* 28.3, 30.1, and above n. 4). In consequence of the great flood of 54 B.C. (Dio Cass. 39.61.1-2, 63.3) the censors of that year took charge of the repairs from upstream of the Pons Mulvius in the north to the "Almone" (cf. Cic. *Ad Q. Fr.* 3.5.8) well south of St. Paul's outside the Walls (Lugli, *ibid.*, pp. 69-72). See below.

[15]See above, nos. 7 and 12. These gladiatorial combats smack of funeral rites for the dead Drusus.

[16]Suet. *Aug.* 57.1, without reference to their locations.

[17]Galen *Libr. Propr.* 19.8 K., *Praen.* 14.620 K., 625 K.; Gellius *NA* 18.4.1; *CIL* VI 448, 761; *Bull. Comm.* 1877, p. 162. The inscribed bases in chronological order are *CIL* VI 30974 (to Mercurius in 10 B.C.), 457 (to Volcanus in 9 B.C.), 458 (to a deity whose name is lost, in 8 B.C.), and 456 (to the Lares Publici in 4 B.C.); *AE* 1980, no. 56 (see S. Panciera, "Nuovi luoghi di culto a Roma," in *Quaderni del centro di studio per l'archeologia etrusco-italica* 4 (1980) [= *Archeologia Laziale* 3] pp. 205-206) to another deity whose name is lost in A.D. 10. Moreover, *magistri vici* themselves dedicated to Stata Fortuna Augusta on 1 January A.D. 12 (VI 761). The canonical, but perhaps too rigidly applied, year 7

known. Indeed the god is barely attested. Lucian entitled one of his wittiest dialogues after Zeus Tragoidos. Some of the dialogue and a description of tragic actors in divine roles suffice to render an idea of what we might have expected if we had gazed at Jupiter the Tragic Player.[18]

The presentation to Jupiter of *ludi votivi* for Augustus's return at the site beneath the Piazza S. Apollinare where the monumental masks were discovered with the record of the games themselves could well have invited Augustus's award of a very costly statue that also promoted at least from 10 B.C. onwards his program of a "neighborhood improvement."[19]

Jupiter's manifestation is attested under unusual circumstances in A.D. 1 in this quarter but not on the very site of the discovery of the masks.

II.3 By Order of Jupiter

About 225 meters north of where the two inscriptions of the votive games and the five monumental masks were discovered was found in 1890 a simple marble tablet whose text has generated much discussion.[20] (See plan 2, no. 1.) Although it lacks some fragments from the upper corners, its purport has remained intelligible. To all appearances it was erected by a *magister vici* who dates his offering both by the consular year of (1 January to 30 June) A.D. 1 and by the neighborhood's era, year nine, evidently as a New Year's offering. Accordingly, the compital era of this neighborhood commenced in 8 B.C., the year when games for Augustus's return were given somewhere near or on the Caelian Hill (see above, II.1). This foundation date may reflect Augustus's building program for this zone in consequence of flooding. Although at least twelve divinities (to whom three were later added) received the dedication, it was prompted by the bidding of only one of them, Jupiter. The place where it was found lies at the downstream end

---

B.C. for the organization and founding of the fourteen regions and the neighborhoods (*vici*) is found in Dio Cass. 55.8.6-7.

[18]An Apollo Sandaliarius was apparently a statue naked except for sandals (cf. Paus. 7.20.3). Although Lucian entitled his dialogue after Zeus Tragoidos we can only glean from one passage what his statue might have looked like (*Jup. Trag.* 41), and Jupiter Tragoedus remains a virtually obscure god.

[19]According to the Tabula Hebana, lines 50-54, the Ludi Augustales of October included theatrical games at least under Tiberius. These games preceded the Augustalia on 12 October, a holy day occasioned by Augustus's return in 19 B.C. and the innovation of the cults of Fortuna Redux; see Degrassi (above, no. 2) pp. 516, 519-520. Theater was also presented in the urban *vici*; see Suet. *Jul.* 39.1, *Aug.* 43.1.

[20]*CAR* I-I, 47, p. 105; *CIL* VI 30975 = *ILS* 3090. It was found more or less by the ancient river embankment.

of the Lungotevere Marzio where the Via di Monte Brianzo joins it. In a word it stood on the Tiber River embankment.

In the following text the italicized names of three divinities in lines 1 and 17 are thought to be additions and those in line 17 later than that of line 1.[21]

> *Mercurio*
> aeterno deo Io[vi]
> [I]unoni Regin(ae), Min[ervae],
> [So]li, Lunae, Apol[lini],
> 5 [Dia]nae, Fortuna[e, Iunoni]
> [Luci]nae, Opi, Isi Pe[lagiae],
> [_ ± _7_] *v* Fati{i}s D[ivinis],
> [quod bo]num [faustum]
> [*vacat* feli]xque [siet *vacat*]
> 10 imp(eratori) Caesari Augus[to, Genio]
> eius, senati populi[q(ue) Romani],
> et gentibus, nono [anno]
> intro eunte felic[iter *vacat*]
> C(aio) Caesare L(ucio) *vacat* Pau[llo co(n)s(ulibus)],
> 15 L(ucius) Lucretius L(uci) l(ibertus) Zethus
> iussu Iovis aram Augustam
> *Salus Semonia* posuit *Populi Victoria*

Before appending a brief commentary to the text, I recall that the votive games for Jupiter on behalf of the return of Augustus were held nearby and the hypothesis that Augustus had given a statue of Jupiter the Tragic Player to a neighborhood in this sector. In this inscription Jupiter has bidden Lucretius give the August altar not merely to himself but to the other two divinities of the Capitoline triad, Juno and Minerva, then to the two pairs of Sun and Moon and of Apollo and Diana and, as I will suggest, to another divine pair of Isis and one of her male associates.

As we now know, Mommsen at first believed that the inscription was to be related to the newly discovered fragments of the proceedings of the Secular Games, discovered some 650 meters to the west of this find, and also by the Tiber bank.[22] Of the gods to whom Lucretius Zethus dedicated the altar, Fortuna and Isis (with a male divinity?) cannot be

---

[21]*CIL* VI 30975; see in the last place, M. A. Cavallaro, "Un liberto 'prega' per Augusto e per le *gentes*: *CIL* VI 30975 (con inediti di Th. Mommsen)," *Helikon* 15-16 (1975-1976): 146-186, a lengthy discussion of some aspects of this text. It contains the earlier bibliography on the text. On p. 151 she supplies a fine photograph that I have used to calculate the number of missing letters. Nota bene: the size and height of letters diminish as the text progresses; some letters now missing were earlier read as extant.

[22]See Cavallaro (note, 21), 155-156, quoting Mommsen's correspondence. For the find-sites of the *acta* of the *Ludi Saeculares* see *CAR* I-H, 96 and 120, pp. 91, 97; some more fragments were found in 1930. These are the only firm indications of the site of the Tarentum where the altar of Dis and Proserpina was buried. See Plan 2.

directly attributed to the Secular Games or to their related ceremonies. Of those attributed divinities only Ops perhaps did not receive cult, but in this text she may stand in for the absent and important Terra Mater.

For the deities and rites of the Secular Games we are especially well informed. Fragments of the inscribed proceedings of Augustus's ceremonies in 17 B.C. survive; to a very slight extent fragments of the inscribed proceedings of Claudius's ceremonies in A.D. 47 were found in the nineteenth century; and, to a great extent the lengthy *acta* of the ceremonies of Septimius Severus and Caracalla, held in A.D. 204, were found in both 1890-91 and 1930. In addition, Domitian issued coins illustrating his Secular Games. The Severan emperors and Philip the Arab would follow suit. Besides these documents of an official kind we have the two Augustan poems of Horace: his famous Secular Hymn and the ode he wrote on the rehearsal of the chorus for the performance of the Hymn.[23]

Comment on *CIL* VI 30975

Line 1. See on line 17.

Line 2. Aeterno deo. The nearest analogue comes from the Feriale Cumanum (A.D. 4-14) wherein the supplication commemorating Augustus's first assumption of the *fasces* was made to *Iovi Sempi[terno].*[24] The pontiffs were said to pray *Iuppiter optime maxime sive quo alio nomine te appellari volueris.*[25] *Aeternus* and *sempiternus* were probably attached to Jupiter because of his heavenly realm since the word *aeternus* had been previously used to describe the augural sections of the sky.[26] In the proceedings of the Augustan games are met entire or partly restored words of prayer addressed to the several gods *uti . . . incolumitatem sempiternam, victoriam, valetudinem p. R. Quiritibus duis* or *duitis.*[27] After the deification of the dead Augustus he is associated on a coin of Spanish Tarraco with a temple of the *Aeternitas Augusta.*[28] This new notion may be derived from Jupiter's prior eternity or from the eternity of the Roman "name."[29] Horace expressed the notion by attributing to Apollo *remque Romanam Latiumque felix,/ alterum in lustrum meliusque semper/*

---

[23]For all these texts and others see I.B. (G.B.) Pighi, *De Ludis Saecularibus populi Romani Quiritium,* 2nd ed. (Amsterdam 1965). For Horace, the *Carmen Saeculare,* and the rehearsal Ode 4.6 we have the jewel of learning that is the seventh chapter of E. Fraenkel, *Horace* (Oxford 1957). Also see below, n. 33.

[24]Degrassi (above, n. 2) pp.279, 392. In the Feriale Amerinum the apparently coordinate sacrifice of five victims was made *Io/vi O(ptimo) M(aximo);* see Degrassi, p. 389.

[25]Serv. *Aen.* 2.351.

[26]Varro *LL* 6.11, *hinc poetae, aeterna templa caeli.* See *Thes. Lingu. Lat.*s.v. *aeternitas,* cols. 1139-1140, *aeternus,* cols. 1142-1144. Of course, the later Jupiter *deus aeternus* who is the oriental *ba'al,* Dolichenus, should not be confused with the older Roman notion.

[27]Pighi (above, n. 23), 114-116.

[28]V. Ehrenberg and A. H. M. James, *Documents Illustrating the Reigns of Augustus and Tiberius,* 2nd ed. Oxford 1955, no. 107a.

[29]*ILS* 157.

prorogat aevom.[30] In the *acta* of the Secular Games Jupiter is always given
his epithets *Optimus Maximus,* as also in the records of the votive games
for Augustus's return, but on this inscription the epithets are omitted.
This is worth emphasizing for the reason that Juno's epithet *Regina* is
not omitted since, I argue below, she also appears in the text as Juno
Lucina. The Secular sacrifices for Jupiter Best and Greatest occurred
on the Capitol.[31]

Line 3. Juno Regina received Secular sacrifice also on the Capitol after
Jupiter.[32] Minerva has an uncertain place in any of the several surviving
accounts and records of the Secular Games.[33] Doubtless she also stands
in this text to complete the Capitoline triad. It follows that the Jupiter in
line 2 was considered Optimus Maximus.

Line 4. In none of the surviving lines of the *acta* stands the name of Sol
or Luna, who are counterpoised here to Apollo and Diana. They are
met, however, in Horace.[34] Apart from Augustus's dedication of obe-
lisks, this inscription is the oldest dated dedication to the Sun God in
Rome.[35] Although I consider the presence of the Sun and the Moon
divinities solely attributable to the notions attaching to the Secular
Games, two other factors may contribute to or reinforce their prece-
dence over Apollo and Diana. First of all, there stood little more than
500 meters to the east of this site the obelisk installed as the pointer of
his enormous sundial.[36] (See Plan 1.) Second, and perhaps coinciden-
tally, the Roman moneyer, L. Lucretius Trio minted in 76 B.C. a denar-
ius whose obverse exhibited the radiate head of the Sun and reverse the
lunar crescent surrounded by seven stars. The stars refer to the constel-
lation of the Triones and make the moneyer's *type parlant.*[37] It would be
an act of deep faith to link directly the freedman L. Lucretius Zethus
with L. Lucretius Trio nearly eighty years earlier. But Apollo and his
sister Diana, restored in the next Line 5, are amply documented in the

---

[30]*Carm. Saec.* 66-68. *Aevom* is the stem of *aeternus.*

[31]Pighi (above, n. 23), 132, 301-302.

[32]Ibid., 132, 302-303.

[33]L. Moretti, "Frammenti vecchi e nuovi del Commentario dei Ludi Secoloare del 17
a.C." *Pont. Accad. Rom. Arch. Rend.,* ser. 3, 55-56. (1982-1984=1985), 362-379, esp. pp.
370ff., restores the name of Minerva in newly published fragments of the Augustan proceedings of the Secular Games that lengthen the list of deities concerned with the names
of Latona, Mars and Hercules Victores, and Jupiter Stator, as well as Apollo, Diana, and
Latona.

[34]*Carm. Saec.* 35-36, cf. *Carm.* 4.6. Phlegon of Tralles quotes the Sibyl's prophecy link-
ing Apollo and Helios (lines 16-18; see Pighi, above, n. 23, p. 57), but that is a witness
over a century later than the inscription.

[35]S. Panciera, "Iscrizioni senatorie di Roma e dintorni," *Titulus* 4.1 (1982), 594-596,
dates to the Augustan period a base sacred to the Sun and Apollo on the grounds of the
dedicant's name and relates the dedication to the notion of identifying Apollo and the Sun
that was born in the first emperor's reign.

[36]See E. Buchner, "Solarium Augusti und Ara Pacis," *Roem. Mitt.* 83 (1976): 319-373 &
"Horologium Solarium. Vorbericht über die Ausgrabungen 1979/80," ibid. 87 (1980):
355-373 = *Die Sonnenuhr des Augustus* (Mainz 1982); idem, "Horologium Augusti," *Gym-
nasium* 90 (1983): 494-508.

[37]M. H. Crawford, *Roman Republican Coinage,* 2 vols. (Cambridge 1974) no. 390/1.

proceedings and the poetry of the Secular Games. Joint sacrifice was made to them on the Palatine Hill.[38] Fortuna is not found in the accounts or records of the Secular ceremonies. Space permits restoration of *Junoni/Lucilnae*. By the two epithets she is here distinguished from Juno Regina of line 3. Uniformly her Greek counterpart receives the nocturnal sacrifice at the Tiber river under the guise of the (plural) Ilithyiae.[39] As a singular goddess Horace addresses her as Ilithyia, Lucina and Genitalis, presiding over childbirth.[40] Normally the name Lucina cannot stand alone for Juno Lucina. *Genitalis* is unparalleled but functionally suits the poet's needs.

Line 6. The goddess Ops apparently has no cult in the Secular Games but is recorded in fragments of the Augustan games for an occurrence *ad aedem] Opis in Capitolio.*[41] Mother Earth, Terra Mater, had an elaborate nocturnal cult with offering of a pregnant sow.[42] Perhaps in functional notion she is here represented by Plenty.[43] If one hesitates to underscore the dedication to the Sun by referring to the obelisk of the solarium, one cannot evade the outright Egyptianness of Isis. That she is here a local goddess can be inferred from the discovery of a dedication to Harpocrates, also on the Tiber embankment, more or less 240 meters west of this inscription.[44] (See Plan 2, no. 2.) To donate a figure of her baby Horus, also named Harpocrates, to Isis seems to have been normal.[45] I have restored Isis's marine epithet *Pe/lagiae.*[46] A freedman of

---

[38]Pighi (above, n. 23), 303-304; Moretti (above, n. 33), 374-379; Hor. *Carm. Saec.* and *Carm.* 4.6.

[39] Pighi (above, n. 23), 302. Huelsen on *CIL* VI 30975 reports earlier suggestions of *Matris Mag/nae* and *Lato/nae*. The latter does not complete line 5 and the former, adopted by Cavallaro, is odd when one would expect *Matri deum Magnae* (with or without *Idaeae* following). For late and ambiguous evidence of Lucina in this area see below, n. 219. Moretti (above, n. 33), 374-379, now provides (from lines 9-10 of the new fragment of the Secular proceeding) *Appollinem Latonam Dianam matremq(ue)/ [deum magnam* etc. He bases his restoration of the Mater Deum Magna on *CIL* VI 30975 which he implicitly links to the Secular deities. Further he rejects Mater Terra as abnormal order. At lines 5-6 of *CIL* VI 30975 there does not seem to be space for the necessary *Matri deum Mag/nae*.

[40]*Carm. Saec.* 13-24. Juno Lucina is named in the Severan proceedings at I 18 (Pighi, p. 141) and in its choral hymn (ibid., 222-224, on Va 63).

[41]*Acta Lud. Quint.*, lines 74-75, on Pighi, 113. If the text were sound it might reveal a sacrifice, e.g. *aram/ Opis*. There is no sign of Ops in the Severan proceedings.

[42]Pighi (above, n. 23), 303; Hor. *Carm. Saec.* 29-32 (*Tellus*). See above, n. 39.

[43]Ops might stand for Terra (Macr. *Sat.* 1.10.18-22) though the underlying notion is that of the Hellenic Rhea; see G. Wissowa, *Religion and Kultus der Römer,* 2nd ed. (Munich 1912) 203-204.

[44]*NdSc* 1898, p. 64 = *CIL* VI 35404; marble slab from Tor di Nona that reads—*rpocrati*. See *CAR* I-I 72, p. 110. In the *CIL* the name is hesitantly taken as personal *Ha/rpocrati/on*, on the assumption that it might be a tombstone. Inscribed tombstones in this sector are plotted on *CAR* I-I 88, 96, 124.

[45]See *CIL* VI 2796 = *ILS* 4372; cf. *IGUR* 177; *CIL* VI 31. The altar dedicated only to Isis and found in the remains of the Iseum of the Campus Martius bears a relief of Harpocrates and of Anubis. See H. Stuart Jones, *Catalogue of the Museo Capitolino* (Rome 1912), 359.

[46]Both the drawing in *NdSc* 1890, p. 285, and the photograph published by Cavallaro (above, n. 21) permit a reading of I or E. Dessau, *ILS* 3090, proposed *Pi/etati*, hesitantly. Huelsen, *CIL* VI 30975, shows a clear part of an I or L.

the emperor Galba (d. A.D. 69) was the warder of a Roman temple of Isis Pelagia,[47] whose whereabouts remain unknown. Isis Pelagia protected sailors whose cult is thought to have reached Rome as early as Augustus's reign.[48] The fact remains that a dock for ships may have lain in this district at the time of this inscription[49] so that the cult of Isis Pelagia would have served the sector well.[50] More pertinently Isis, especially if represented with her baby, would fit in the series of Fortuna, and Juno Lucina protecting parturition and maternity.

Line 7. Although an empty letter space stands before F, seven letters could have been carved in the line before the break on the left. Because we have the pairs Sol and Luna, and Apollo and Diana, I would suppose that after *Isi Pe[lagiae* was carved the name of *Serapi* or *Osiri* or *Horo* (*Harpocrati* would have been too long). The *Fata D[ivina* stand here for the Moerae of the Secular proceedings and the Parcae in Horace's choral hymn who, like the Ilithyiae and Terra Mater, received nocturnal sacrifice by the Tiber bank.[51] The Fata Divina were later illustrated in a remarkable tomb on the Appian Way along with the lord of the Underworld. The text, belonging to the tomb of a wife of a priest of Sabazius, has legends identifying the painted figures adorning the chamber: Dis Pater, Aeracura, Fata Divina, Mercurius Nuntius, Vibia (the deceased), Alcestis, abreptio Vibies et discensio, septe(m) pii sacerdotes . . . , bonorum iudicio iudicati, Vibia, angelus bonus, inductio Vibies.[52] These sepulchral fancies recall the universally acknowledged fact that the Secular Games were derived from the cult of Dis and Proserpina (here Aeracura, we presume) at the Tarentum. Yet there is not a single trace of either deity in the inscribed proceedings.[53] In Vibia's tomb Aeracura, whoever she was,[54] stands by Dis as Proserpina does in accounts of the Tarentum of the Secular Games. The painting of the

---

[47]*CIL* VI 8707 = *ILS* 4421. Although temple warders were otherwise normally imperial freedmen, the man or Galba himself may have had a special relationship to Isis if the name of Ser. Sulpicius Aug. 1. Horus (*CI* VI 26959) is significant.

[48]Tib. 1.3.22-34, by no means a clear proof of Pelagia's arrival.

[49]I am referring to the so-called mole at Tor di Nona (see plan 2.); see D. Marchetti, *NdSc* 1890, p. 153 (notice, too, of a lead pipe inscribed with the name of Claudius); *Bull. Comm.* 1891, pp. 45-69 (with discussion of its serving the traffic in marbles); *NdSc* 1892, pp. 110-111. A recent discussion of the dock and its temple, attributed to Hercules, is that of E. La Rocca, *La riva a mezzaluna* (Rome 1984), 57-69. On a later nearby dock see below, sect. II.9.

[50]An Isis temple by the sea or a river port would seem appropriate. See Apul. *Metam.* 11.5; Pausanias 2.4.7; R. Meiggs, *Ostia*, 2nd ed. (Oxford 1973), 368-370. In his restoration of the Iseum of the Campus Martius Domitian symbolically linked the two famous rivers by installing two elaborate statues of the Nile (now in the Vatican) and of the Tiber . (formerly in the Vatican, now in the Louvre.) See P. P. Bober and R. Rubenstein *Renaissance Artists and Antique Sculpture*, (Oxford 1986), 99-105, nos. 66-67, for the history of these pieces.

[51]Pighi (above, n. 23), 299-301; Hor. *Carm. Saec.* 25-28.

[52]*CIL* VI 142 = *ILS* 3961. The name *M. Aur[elius* surely suggests a Severan date.

[53]Pighi (above, n. 23), 33-62.

[54]See Wissowa (above, n. 43) p. 313; *ILS* 3960-3968. Where a dedication for Dis Pater occurs, either Aeracura or Proserpina, never both, may also be met.

Fata Divina shows three figures, one a bearded male. In a dedication to the same Fata three pairs of feet remain on the *ex viso*.[55] The fourth divinity commemorated in the tomb was Mercurius Nuntius, that is the well-known Hermes Psychopompus. Mercury is the god whose name was later made to head the text of our inscribed tablet.[56]

Line 10. After *Augus/to* have been restored various nouns in the dative case that would control *eius* (sc. *Augusti*), *senati* and *populi*. They are *tutelaeque* (Barnabei, Mommsen), *curae* (Mommsen's alternative), *imperio* (Von Premerstein, Huelsen, and Cavallaro in a different sense).[57] With some reluctance I propose the restoration *Genio]/eius* etc.[58] The dative nouns *Caesari*, [*Genio*], and *gentibus* depend on the prayer, "May it be good, blessed and fortunate for Caesar, for his Genius, the Genius of the Senate and the Genius of Roman People, and for the Nations." In the famous inscription from Narbo of the year A.D. 11 by which the cult of the Numen Augusti was founded we have the opening of the prayer: "quod bonum faustum felixque sit imp. Caesari divi f. Augusto . . . , coniugi liberis gentique eius, senatui populoque Romano . . ."[59] Our choices, it seems to me, are three. First, adopt the *genti* and retain all three genitives *eius*, *senati*, and *populi*. Second, adopt *genti* and correct *senati* and *populi* to the dative case. Third, seek another noun for restoration as all others before me have done. The nearest to retaining both the underlying notion of the close parallel Narbonese text and the readings of this inscription is to adopt *genio*, related to the idea of *gens* as well as some of the progenerative functions inhering in the goddesses whose names have preceded this clause. In inscriptions put up by *magistri vici* are often met dedications *Laribus Augustis et Genis Caesarum*.[60] Dedication to Augustus's *genius* occurs late in his reign[61] and is briefly kept for Tiberius.[62] Of course, the *Genius populi Romani* or *Genius publicus* is much older than the Genius of the emperor.[63] What lies in the path of acceptance of the restoration *genio* is *genio] senati*. Though it is imaginable for African town councils,[64] the Genius of the Roman Senate is first publicly acknowledged on the coins of Antoninus Pius.[65] Rather lamely I can but excuse the ineptitude of L. Lucretius Zethus or commend his inventiveness by analogy.

---

[55]*CIL* VI 145 = 30701: Fatis Divinis C. Clod[ius—]anus/ ex viso vo[tu]m solvit.

[56]See below, sect. II.11.

[57]See Cavallaro (above, n. 21), 157-163.

[58]Cavallaro, p. 159, n. 56, considered and rejected *geniis*.

[59]*CIL* XII 4333 = *ILS* 112.

[60]*CIL* VI 445, 449, 451, 452, 30958; *AE* 1971, no. 34; cf. Ovid *Fasti* 5.129-158. Also see below, nn. 61, 62 and 71.

[61]*CIL* XI 3076 = *ILS* 116: Genio Augusti et Ti. Caesaris, Iunoni Liviae Mystes l.

[62]*CIL* VI 251 = 30724 = *ILS* 6080. Put up in A.D. 27 by a *magister pagi*. Also see E. De Ruggiero, *Dizionario Epigrafico*, vol. 3, pp. 458ff., for the Genius Augusti.

[63]See Wissowa (above, n. 43), 179-180; De Ruggiero (above, n. 62), 467-468.

[64]De Ruggiero (above, n. 62), 468.

[65]See *TLL*, s.v. Genius, 1833, 66ff. See H. Mattingly, *Coins of the Roman Empire in the British Museum* vol. 4 (London 1968), 879-880 (of the index vol.). For an author's mention we must wait for Cassiodorus *Varia* 1.4.1, 3.6.2 when the Senate counted for nothing

Line 12. That Zethus engaged in unique thinking seems proved by *gentibus*. What he means by clans or nations or, as some would have it, provinces has not been ascertained.[66] Tortured as it is, the *gentes* may stand for the "world," the *orbis terrarum*, with a play on the *etymon* of *genius* and *gens*. In line 13 *felic[iter* reminds us of the phrase in the Narbonese inscription speaking of Augustus's birthday *qua die eum saeculi felicitas orbi terrarum rectorem edidit*,[67] "the day when the blessedness of the era brought him forth as the guide of the world."

Lines 12-14. The ninth year is reckoned by the compital era when Augustus reorganized the cult of Compital Lares as August Lares.[68] The word *introeunte* (written here as two words) recalls Augustus's conversion of New Years's gifts to costly statues for the neighborhoods.[69] L. Aemilius Paullus was consul only till 1 July A.D. 1.

Line 15. Although he bears no title, Zethus seems to have been one of the four annual *magistri* of this neighborhood.[70]

Line 16. The Jupiter who enjoined establishment of the altar to all these gods is the Jupiter Tragoedus, whose statue I suggested was given to the neighborhood, or Jupiter Best and Greatest to whom the votive games for Augustus's return were dedicated. The altar is described as *Augusta*, another sign that it is furniture for a compital shrine.[71] Not 76 meters from the tablet was found an elaborately carved altar in the church of S. Lucia della Tinta. (See Plan 2, no. 4.) It is unusual in being the only altar found in Rome with the single word *sacrum* without the name of its deity.[72] I would urge that this one altar stood for all the deities listed in our tablet, too numerous to mention on the altar.

---

in the Empire. (Compare the uncertain passage in Rut. Namat. *Red.* 1.13-19.) The appearance of the *Genius Senatus* is dated as early as the Flavian dynasty by F. Beranger, "Les Génies du senat et du Peuple Romain et les reliefs flaviens de la Cancelleria," *Principatus* (Geneva, 1973), 399-410 and by H. Kunckel, *Der römische Genius = Röm. Mitt.* Suppl. vol. 20 (1974) pp. 37 ff., who base themselves on sculptural iconography. Explicit mention of the *Genius Senatus* is no older than Antoninus Pius unless my restoration be accepted.

[66]Cavallaro, (above, n. 21), 163-173, discusses the term at length, partly in light of her understanding of her reading *imperio] eius, senati populique*.

[67]See above, n. 59.

[68]See above, n. 17 and below, n. 71, for references to other inscriptions marking compital eras, and Cavallaro (above, n. 21), 177-181. Probably Augustus founded this neighborhood in fact since the whole sector could have undergone building only after the establishment of flood control.

[69]See above, sect. II.2, and n. 17.

[70]Cavallaro, ibid. The suggestion is Dessau's.

[71]Cavallaro (above, n. 21), 173-177. Compare the application of the epithet *augustus* in these compital dedications, a selection from CIL VI: Aisculapio Augusto (12 = 30684, year 31), Apollini Aug. (33, year 6), Mercurio Aug. (34, year 5), Apollini Aug. (35, year 52), Dianae Aug. (129, year 7), Mercurio Aug. (283, year 1; cf. 282), Herculi Tutatori Aug. (342 = 30743, year 32), Laribus Aug., Genis Caesarum (445, year 1), L.A. (446, 447, year 1), L.A. (448), L.A. et G.C. (449, year 92, making a foundation of 9 B.C.), L.A. (451, year at least 106 in AD 100), L.A. et G.C. (452, year 121 in A.D. 109), L.A. (30957), year 9), L.A. (36809, year 6), Statae Matri Aug. (764, year 2), S.M.A. (766, year 50), Volcano Quieto Aug. (801, year at least 50), V.Q.A. et S.M.A. (802, year 5), Veneri Aug. (*AE* 1980, n. 54, year 3, from the same man mentioned in 282, 283).

[72]*CIL* VI 31073; *CAR* I-I, 59, p. 108. I assert its uniqueness by reference only to the

Line 17. The words *Salus Semonia* and *Populi Victoria* (in the nominative case) as well as the *Mercurio* of line 1 (in the dative case), are owed to one or, more likely, two subsequent carvings.[73] Mercury might be honored anywhere.[74] Salus Semonia is found otherwise only once in an alphabetical list and her function remains totally obscure.[75] The proclamation of Populi Victoria seems antithetical to the many later dedications made throughout the empire to Victoria Caesaris.

To recapitulate the substance of the suggested relationship between this peculiar text and the Secular ceremonies, we recall that aside from the ever absent Dis and Proserpina, all the gods and goddesses who were worshipped at the Secular ceremonies are met on this dedication except Terra Mater. She may be represented here by Ops, by whose Capitoline temple (?) some Secular observance was marked in 17 B.C. Sol and Luna, an analogue of sorts to Apollo and Diana, are met only in Horace's reflection on the rites. Minerva (perhaps), Fortuna, Isis Pelagia and her restored male cult-partner have no connection with the Secular Games. From a presumed dedication to Harpocrates found in the sector we infer that Isis protected the local port and its shipping.

But the Secular deities discussed here had no permanent altars for obvious reasons. They were given sacrifice on temporary altars. The altar or altars of Dis and Proserpina lay at a depth of twenty feet below grade and were uncovered only every century or century plus ten years when the extraordinary rites were required.[76] Among the rites and distinct from the sacrifice given by Augustus and the Severi were counted the stage plays and the chariot races, as well as other circus business. In fact, only these activities constituted the *ludi* proper.

The protocol of setting up some temporary structures for stage plays and races is noted in the Augustan *acta* and is later observed likewise by the Severans. At the Tiber on the Campus where the Moerae had just received sacrifice: "games were given at night on the stage to which no theater had been added and no seats were placed."[77] After the sacrifices to Jupiter (in daylight) "the Latin plays were given in the wooden theater which had been set up on the Campus along the Tiber."[78] The so-

---

computerized index of *CIL* VI, fasc. 7, where no other dedication has so bald a text.

[73]See Cavallaro (above, n. 21), 149-152. The different cases strongly suggest a second and third occasion.

[74]But see above on line 7.

[75]See Wissowa (above, n. 43), 131-132; E. Norden, *Aus altroemischen Priesterbuechern, Acta Reg. Soc. Hum. Litt. Lundensis* 29 (1939): 204-213.

[76]On the altars of the Underworld pair see Zosimus 2.1-5, Val. Max. 2.4.5, Festus, 440 L.; for the temporary altars recorded in the inscribed Severan proceedings see III 69, Va 47, Va 53-54, (Pighi, 154, 162, 163).

[77]*Acta*, lines 100-101, Pighi, p. 114. Earlier than the structures for the Augustan Secular Games was a temporary stadium built by Julius Caesar in the Campus Martius for athlete contests (Suet. *Jul.* 39.3-4). Its location is unknown. Otherwise, for the spate of theater building in this era see the survey of G. Bejor, "L'edificio teatrale nell' urbanizzazione augustea," *Athenaeum*, 57 (1979): 126-138.

[78]*Acta*, line 108, Pighi, 115.

called honorary (i.e. supplementary) games were held as follows: Latin plays "in the wooden theater which is at the Tiber," the Greek "thymelic" plays in the Theater of Pompey, and the Greek "astic" plays at the theater in the Circus Flaminius.[79] The last was that theater we call by the name of Marcellus. As for the races and like games, they were held "next to that place where sacrifice had been done on the previous nights and where the theater had been set and there is a stage, turning posts were set and fourhorse cars were raced etc."[80]

Although more complex, the testimony of the Severan *acta* amply affirms what had been done 220 years earlier. There was a stage without a theater.[81] The wooden theater stood again for single events and as one of three for the "honorary" plays when it again offered the Latin plays. Pompey's theater was the second of these; Domitian's Music Hall, the Odeum, was the third and offered the Greek plays.[82] The distance to the theater of Marcellus from the center of ceremonies was shortened by transferring the appropriate plays to the Odeum. Although the Severi used the Circus Maximus for some chariot races and beast hunts,[83] they also followed Augustus's protocol and set up a *circus temporalis* with its own starting gate and turning posts for other races and circus entertainment. It evidently rose near the Wooden Theater, that is to say once again along the Tiber.[84]

Evidence for the sites for presenting secular entertainment has been rehearsed at some length because it bears on the situation of the horse exercise ground near the Tarentum. This was called the Trigarium and will occupy the next section of this study.

A wooden theater where Latin plays were presented in daylight stood near where sacrifice was held on the Campus alongside the Tiber. Night games, however, were presented from a stage to an audience supported by neither a theater nor seats, again beside the Tiber. We read of a wooden theater and of no theater. We do not read of a temporary stage (*scaena*) in either case. Indeed, some of the coins commemorating Domitian's Secular Games have long been considered to show numismatic representations of this "temporary" stage.[85] That the coins show

---

[79]*Acta*, lines 156-162, Pighi, 118.

[80]Acta, lines 153-154, Pighi, 118.

[81]*Acta* Va 57 (Pighi, 164); also restored at III 59-60 (Pighi, 153), IV 3 (Pighi, 155).

[82]*Acta* Va 37, Va 43-46, VII 9 (Pighi, 160, 161-162, 170) for the three theaters. For the wooden theater alone see Va 77 (Pighi, 167). Although not presenting the "honorary" plays the theater of Marcellus seems to have been the site of another activity; see III 33 on Pighi, p. 151.

[83]*Acta*, Va 38-43, Pighi, 160-161.

[84]*Acta*, Va 77-83, Pighi, 167-168. Just as the horse leapers were presented in this temporary circus by Augustus (*Acta*, line 154) so, too, the Severi (Va 79-83, every instance restored to the text) also presented them. Pighi, 184, takes the hesitant (*videtur*) view that the Severan temporary circus was constructed for the occasion at the permanent Circus Maximus! A mode of coals to Newcastle, I suppose.

[85]In the last place see La Rocca (above, n. 41), 43-56, also see I. S. Ryberg, *Rites of the State Religion in Roman Art, MAAR* 22 (1955): 174-177. Cf. P. di Manzano, "Note sulla monetazione dei Ludi secolari dell' 88 d. C.," *Bull. Comm.* 89 (1984): 297-304.

two different *scaenae,* if they are *scaenae,* presents a problem only to those who have trouble reading the proceedings. There were doubtless two permanent stages by the Tiber, one without a theater, one with a wooden theater.

The Secular Games had happened eighteen years before Jupiter bade Lucretius Zethus set up the August altar. But in the interval Jupiter Best and Greatest had witnessed in the vicinity the votive games for the return of Augustus, games that must have included stageplays. Otherwise how are we to explain the five monumental theatrical masks found with the inscribed record? If we add to this testimony the suggested installation of Jupiter the Tragic Player in this sector, we can see an avenue of keeping alive the memory of the Secular Games. The place set aside for the stageplays of the Secular Games could have been maintained, at least for a while, so that such votive games could be occasionally presented.

We do not yet have a name for the place which was on the Campus Martius beside the Tiber River. In Jerome's notice of the last Secular Games ever given, those by Philip the Arab, the site of the stageplays is called Field of Ares (Campus Martius) which Castagnoli properly understood as that small field in its narrower sense.[86]

The votive games dedicated to Jupiter for the return of Augustus, the five monumental theatrical masks in marble and Jupiter the Eternal's inscription of a freedman in A.D. 1 testify to occupation of this quarter in the reign of the first emperor. My interpretation is that Augustus himself made the gesture of donating a very costly statue of Jupiter the Tragic Player paid for from the proceeds of his New Year's gifts. On a subsequent New Year's Day, an August altar was dedicated to a peculiarly diverse group of deities. Most of them in fact had received cult only as recently as 17 B.C. during the Secular ceremonies. The dedication itself is remarkable in its being among the oldest explicit Roman offerings to the Sun and to Isis. Implicit in calling the new altar *augusta* is the adherence to another new religious dispensation, one promoted by its very object.

II.4 *Trigarium*

It has been customary to associate some of the Secular Games with a place called the Trigarium whose name recalls the archaic *triga,* a three-horse chariot. The oldest contemporary reference to it falls in the reign

---

[86]Jer. *Chron. a. Abr.* 2262: regnantibus Philippis millesimus annus Romanae urbis expletus est; ob quam solemnitatem innumerabiles bestiae in Circo Magno interfectae, ludique theatrales in Campo Aris per noctem tribus diebus celebrati sunt. See Pighi (above n. 23), 90-94 for the other evidence for these games; Castagnoli (above, n. 12), 146.

of Claudius and the latest occurs in the regionary gazetteers of the
second half of the fourth century.

In his long excursus on the origin of the Tarentine (i.e. Secular)
Games Zosimus, writing ca. A.D. 500, narrates the dream vision of the
children of Valesius, the legendary founder of the rites.[87] In a dream a
tall and god-like man appeared. He enjoined the performance of sacrifice to Dis and Proserpina with dark victims at the Tarentum on the
Field of Mars by which also lay the place for exercising horses.[88] Zosimus, or better his source, imagines that the unknown Tarentum where
the invisible altar will be uncovered can be indicated by reference to an
already existent and visible place called the Trigarium, a word that
would have been unknown to Zosimus' late Greek readers.[89] Consequently, Zosimus defined the landmark. Indeed *trigarium* is one of the
(common) nouns defined in the bilingual glosses as a "place where
horses are exercised."[90] Neither one of these late sources proves the late
antique existence of *the* Roman *trigarium;* one refers to days of legend,
the other defines a common Latin noun for Greeks. Furthermore, neither one of these sources speaks of racing horses, let alone chariots, on
such a ground. In his recent book La Rocca follows Coarelli and makes
extravagant demands on these two sources by claiming that the Trigarium still existed when Zosimus wrote and that it was a racecourse
(*circus, hippodromos*).[91] Both sides in the argument on the locality of the
Trigarium assume that the Trigarium witnessed races for the three annual festivals of Mars and for the Secular Games. On the one hand,
Coarelli and La Rocca would situate a Trigarium of great dimensions
on the western edge of the Campus Martius.[92] On the other, Castagnoli
earlier argued that the Trigarium lay in the vicinity of the Via della

[87]Zosimus, 2.1-7, including the report by Phlegon of the Sibyl's oracle (2.6). Some of
Zosimus's account is paralleled by that of Valerius Maximus 2.4.5. See Pighi, 43-58.
Phlegon was perhaps the direct source used by Zosimus for composing the section on the
Secular Games; see Paschoud *RE* 10A (1972) cols. 813-814.

[88]Zos. 2.2.3: ταῦτα ποιεῖν ἐπισκήψαντος ἐπὶ τοῦ κατὰ Τάραντα 'Αρείου πεδίου, καθ' ὃ
καὶ ἀνεῖται τόπος εἰς γυμνάσιον ἵππων. Mendelssohn inserted νῦν before ἀνεῖται but
Paschoud in the Budé text does not follow him. Valerius Maximus (last note) gives a like
account but mentions neither the Tarentum nor exercise ground.

[89]In the parallel account of Valerius Maximus the father Valerius wants to go buy an
altar in the city, a detail implying a developed community with a *trigarium*.

[90]*Corp. Gloss. Lat.* 2.201. *Trigaria* were not found only at Rome; see *CIL* VIII 16566, the
sepulchral stone of a charioteer of Theveste: nunc requiescunt reliquiae tri[g]ari solo per
quod fui notus. For a treatment of the entire inscription see J. Kolendo, "L'iscrizione di
un auriga a Theueste (*ILAlg.* I 3146)," *L'Africa Romana* 2 (1985): 195-200.

[91]La Rocca (above, n. 49) pp. 57ff. and *passim*, who goes so far as to usurp on p. 58, a
reference to the Circus Maximus as the *hippodromos* in Dio Cassius 56.27.4, which Castagnoli, (above, n.12), 140, should have forestalled; also see Coarelli (below, n. 92). See
my review of La Rocca's book in *Amer. Journ. Arch.*, 92 (1988): 618-619. Were it not for
the fact that the fable comes from Aesop (no. 343 = *Fab. Syn.* 49 Hausrath-Hunger)
proponents of the later existence of the Trigarium as a riding-ground might take solace
from Avianus's fable no. 10 (*de calvo equite*).

[92]F. Coarelli, "Il Campo Marzio occidentale. Storia e topografia", *Mel. Ecole Franç.
Rome* 89 (1977): 839-842, 845. La Rocca (above n. 49), 57ff. and passim.

Scrofa, that is north of Piazza Navona, by the Field of Mars in its limited sense.[93]

It is important to remember that both the Augustan and Severan proceedings of the Secular Games, those given every 100 or 110 years, explicitly tell us that the races were held on a temporarily arranged course, just as the wooden theater was very likely a temporary structure. The annual festivals of Mars called for chariot races three times a year. Until the thoroughgoing imperial administration took in hand control of the Tiber banks there could have been no thought of a permanent racecourse anywhere at all beside the Tiber. Indeed flooding of the plain has continued for centuries.

In 1948 Castagnoli adduced the texts of the votive games for Jupiter discussed above in Section II.1 and the five monumental masks to include the quarter of S. Apollinare in the "small" Campus Martius which he argued was an open and free area available for games, plays and races.[94] To his views, and not to the groundless views of Coarelli and La Rocca, one may subscribe with qualification, although I cannot chart the Trigarium because it was an empty space which has left only one "shadow" reflection.[95]

Our oldest reference to the Trigarium is met in the inscription of a Tiber bank marker found at the church of S. Biagio della Pagnotta and datable to the reign of Claudius. Its provenience has been the sheet anchor of Coarelli and La Rocca charting the Trigarium in the western Campus Martius.[96] We saw that the markers of Tiber bank maintenance might extend for miles along *both* banks.[97] Location of the Trigarium by this single, solitary marker, palpably one of many, is groundless. Moreover, Castagnoli and others knew the marker and never dreamed of using it to establish the two terminal points and proves only that the Trigarium lay on the left river bank.

Pliny the Elder employs the words *trigarium* and *trigarius* in different senses. One is the generic use of *trigarium* in the plural as training grounds.[98] The second gives an extended sense of *trigarius* (*sic*) as trainer of stageplayers and horses, making his exit from the audience.[99] Lastly,

---

[93]Castagnoli (above n. 12), 136, 140-148.

[94]Ibid.

[95]See below, sect. II.8 on the new forum of Sibidius. One must bear in mind that in the regionary gazetteers Campus Martius and Trigarium are two distinct entries; see below, at n. 105.

[96]*CIL* VI 31545 = *ILS* 5926. The five superintendants of the Tiber banks and bed maintained the bank from the Trigarium to the bridge of Agrippa after setting up markers (*cippi*). This is the only reference to the Pons Agrippae. The Pons Agrippae very probably was designed to carry the Aqua Virgo, Agrippa's aqueduct that came to the Saepta in the Campus Martius, across the Tiber to Region XIV; see Front. *Aqu.* 2.84. See La Rocca (above, n. 49) and Coarelli (above, n. 92).

[97]See above, nn. 13-14.

[98]Pliny *NH* 37.202: *equos in trigariis.* Note the absence of chariots. See Kolendo (above, n. 90).

[99]Idem, 29.9; perhaps the collocation of *histriones* and *equi* refer specifically to *the* Triga-

Pliny writes of some (disgusting) medication adopted by charioteers and cites a liquid that Nero usually refreshed himself with when he wanted also to test himself at driving.[100] The sum of the Plinian evidence merely reinforces what the glossator tells us.[101]

Next we have a specific use of Trigarium in a sepulchral text marking the tomb of a man *qui egit officinas plumbarias Tra(n)stiberina (regione) et Trigari, superposito auri monetae num(m)ulariorum,*[102] "who operated lead processing plants in Trastevere and at the Trigarium, (being) superintendent of the coiners of the gold mint." One would have expected an entrepreneur in lead fabrication to have had a relation with a silver mint, not a gold mint. At all events, this man's plant at the Trigarium was doubtless so situated as to take advantage of proximity to a river quay. The most productive activity of a lead plant presumably would have been concentrated in the manufacture of water-pipes. Since pipes were usually identified as to the sources of the system or the property they were not ready-made but made to order. At all events, a lead yard would have been larger than most metal works. We do not know the location of a mint in Rome before that founded near the church of S. Clemente on the Caelian Hill after the demolition of the Golden House. Apparently there was a silver mint near the fountain of Trevi.[103] The private occupation of public land at the Trigarium must have been owed to the dead man's performance of a public service for the state mint. Yet it seems equally clear that the sepulchral text assumes that "Trigarium" had become a toponym. Quilici has demonstrated that no adequate open space existed at the western edge of the Campus Martius, and so he has followed others in believing the word Trigarium designated only a place and no longer a horse exercise ground.[104]

The contemporary last mention of the Trigarium is found in the regionary gazetteers. Because they are sometimes adduced to make topographical argument for the locality of the Trigarium and other places to which we return below, I quote the full list for Region IX of the City.[105]

---

rium of Rome but it cannot be assured. For an extraordinary festival of *orchestai* and *hippotrophoi* see Dio Cass. 56.27.4.

[100]Idem, 28.237-238: *cum sic quoque se trigario adprobare vellet.* This *trigario* is *not* ablative of place where; cf. above, no. 98. Here the word means 'training', 'driving, practice', 'exercise'.

[101]See above at n. 99.

[102]*CIL* VI 8461 = *ILS* 1637.

[103]The find-site (fountain of Trevi) lies about 1.4 km due east of the presumed site of the Tarentum; see *CIL* VI 298 = *ILS* 1636: Herculi Augusto sacrum officinatores et nummulari officinarum argentariarum familiae monetari(ae). Hercules as well as Apollo and Fortuna was honored by the minters of the Caelian mint (*CIL* VI 42-44; *ILS* 1634-1635). I am leaving out of consideration a *moneta* at the temple of Juno Moneta. Lead was regularly "coined" as ephemeral tokens.

[104]L. Quilici, "Il Campo Marzio occidentale," *Città e architettura nella Roma imperiale = Analecta Romana Instituti Danici*, Suppl. 10 (1983) 59-85; see esp. p. 75. How La Rocca, (above, n. 49) could acknowledge this work and persist in following Coarelli's work (above n. 92) is not comprehensible.

[105]I follow, more or less, the texts established by A. Nordh, *Libellus de regionibus urbis*

Region VIIII Circus Flaminius continet:

(labcd)   Stabula numero IIII factionum VI
(2ab)   II aedes
(3abc)   Porticum Philippi, Minucias II, veterem et frumentariam
(4)   Cryptam Balbi
(5abc)   Theatra III
              imprimis Balbi qui capit loca $\overline{\text{XIDC}}$
                        Pompei capit loca $\overline{\text{XVIIDLXXX}}$
                        Marcelli capit loca XXD
(6)   Odium capit loca $\overline{\text{XDC}}$
(7)   Stadium capit loca $\overline{\text{XXXLXXXVIII}}$
(8)   Campum Martium
(9)   Trigarium
(10)   Ciconias
(11)   Nixas
(12)   Pantheum
(13abc)   Basilicam Naptuni, Matidies et Marcianes
(14ab)   Templum divi Antonini et columnam coclidem altam
          pedes CLXXXV s., gradus intus habet CCIII,
          fenestras LVI.
(15)   Hadrianium
(16ab)   Thermas Alexandrianas et Agrippianas
(17ab)   Porticum Argonautarum et Meleagri
(18ab)   Iseum et Serapeum
(19)   Minervam Chalcidicam
(20)   Divorum
(21)   Insulam Felicles

The number of items is greater than the number of entries. Nos. 3abc
are all colonnades, the first being unrelated to the second and third,
Nos. 5abc are all theaters, none is near the others. Nos. 6 and 7 the
Odeum and Stadium are adjacent, we believe, and like the theaters here
exhibit their audience capacity. No. 8, Campus Martius, is to be understood in the terms laid down by Castagnoli. No. 9 Trigarium is distinct
from Campus Martius. Nos. 10 and 11 have until recently been thought
of as a single item.[106] Nos. 13abc are all basilicas, but not necessarily
standing together. Nos. 14 and 15 are indeed set side by side because
they are generically alike as temples of deified emperors. Nos. 16ab,
nos. 17ab, nos. 18ab and 19 and 20, are grouped by generic similarity
of public baths, colonnades (again), temples (though all four may have

---

Romae = Acta Instituti Romani Regni Sueciae, series in 8°, 3 (1949) pp. 86-88, but make an
attempt to unite the two gazetteers. Castagnoli (above, n. 12) states or assumes a sequential topographical order in parts of the gazetteer and La Rocca (above, n. 49) cautions
against this practice and proceeds directly to engage in the practice. Some believe that the
spectator capacity of the Circus Flaminius, the name or title of Region IX, has fallen
from the MSS. since for Region XI, Circus Maximus, the *Notitia* has its capacity and the
Curiosum omits it.
    [106]See below, Sects. II.5, II.9.

comprised a single Domitianic complex). In a sense no. 1 is a generic grouping of all the racing stables. Whatever no. 2 signifies it seems to be a generic grouping. In a larger sense, nos. 5abc, 6 and 7, with their capacities, represent a generic group of public places of state entertainment, yet there is not a sign of sequential topographical order in these five items. In fine, of the thirty-five reckonable items only seven (nos. 4, 8-12, 21) are isolated and not demonstrably listed, as it were, generically. Furthermore, on Castagnoli's showing the Campus Martius (no. 8) was free for the Martial races which he and others believe occurred in the Trigarium (no. 9). However, if we account nos. 8 and 9 as public places of occasional state entertainment, we must acknowledge at the same time that the gazetteers give no seating capacity as in the preceding five items, because they offered no permanent seating. Finally, it is true that the Stadium (Piazza Navona) lies immediately south of the Campus Martius, in its narrowest sense and may be considered in a sequential topographical order. (It is empirically impossible for the gazetteer of Region IX to be thought a compilation of all entries in a sequential topographical order.)

At this junction we have not discovered the site of the Trigarium. While it was thought to be older than the republic it is not surely attested before the reign of Claudius. Other than by definition a horse is not known of a certainty to have set hoof on the Roman Trigarium. At some time it held a lead processing establishment assumed to have been close to whatever river quay lay open to lead shipment. In the mid-fourth century it is listed in the gazetteer for Region IX as separate from the Campus Martius.

II.5 Silvanus and the Nixae

In 1978 I treated two shrines of Silvanus from the northern Campus Martius. One was represented by an inscription from the site of the discovery of some of the fragments of the *acta* of the Secular Games and was linked by me to an epigram of Martial mentioning Pan, one of Silvanus' identities, at the Tarentum.[107] The other shrine is evidenced by two inscriptions from the Via degli Acqasparta (see Plan 2, no. 3), one of which was dedicated to Silvanus on 15 October A.D. 170, the Martial feastday of the October Horse. Since the calendar of the mid-fourth century states that this horse was sacrificed *ad Nixas*, I assumed that, given a longstanding relation of Mars and Silvanus, we were entitled to

---

[107]R. E. A. Palmer, "Silvanus, Sylvester, and the Chair of St. Peter," *Proc. Amer. Philos. Soc.* 122 (1978); 239, 245-247. Also see S. Panciera, "Silvano a Roma," forthcoming in studies for Georgi Mihailov.

infer the very site of the Nixae and the proximity of the "Campus Martius" where the horse race had been run.[108]

In his book, La Rocca gives ample reasons to suppose that the Nixae, kneeling women in the act of parturition or kneeling goddesses of that ilk who oversaw childbirth, should be somehow closely related to the Ilithyiae of the Secular proceedings to whom the emperors directed nocturnal prayer and sacrifice by the Tiber.[109] The survey of the archaeological site reveals that the Tarentum was devoid of buildings.[110] (See Plan 2.)

The spot where Silvanus was honored on 15 October A.D. 170 lies 200 meters NW of the find-site of the inscriptions of the earlier votive games for Jupiter and the monumental masks (above, Sect. II.1) and more or less 175 meters SW of the find-site of the August altar ordered by Jupiter for the many gods (above, Sect. II.3).[111] (See Plan 2, no. 3.) In the present state of our knowledge perhaps only one ancient street ran NS to the river from the straightway lying beneath the Via dei Coronari and between the street leading to the Pons Aelius and the street lying beneath the Via della Scrofa.[112] I shall show below how this street paving may be related to construction in late antiquity.[113] Therefore, the races, the stageplays, the ceremonies for Mars could have been performed in this sector by the river at the northern and fluvial limit of the plain and upstream from the elbow-bend in the stream.

The quarter of the Campus Martius witnessed either the sacrifice of the October Horse or the horse race for Mars, or it witnessed both annual events on 15 October.

---

[108]Palmer (above, n. 107), 239-240. I made no effort to distinguish the Nixae from the Ciconiae (see below, sect. II.9). La Rocca, (above, n. 49), has no knowledge of this discussion of the site of the *Nixae* (see next note).

[109]La Rocca (above, n. 49), 57-69 and often passim. I do not agree with La Rocca's attempts to place the *Nixae* where he does (see above, n. 108) and, for that matter, dissent from his and Coarelli's (above, n. 92) situation of both the Trigarium and the Tarentum. I observe the indication of the find-sites of the fragments of the *acta* (*CAR* I-H, 96 and 120, pp. 91, 96-97, cf. Romanelli, *NdSc* 1931, pp. 313-345). Moreover, S. Quilici Gigli, "Estremo Campo Marzio. Alcune osservazioni sulla topografia", *ARID* Suppl. 10 (above, n. 104), 47-58, has shown the importance of the two paved lots near the site of the relevant epigraphic discoveries in terms of an *area* for the Tarentine ceremonies. Coarelli and La Rocca would have us believe that the Tarentum lay due south of the find-sites themselves and the Trigarium south of that Tarentum. Neither my hypothesis on the location of the Nixae (above, n. 107) nor that of La Rocca on the nature of the Nixae was known to J.-M. Flambard, "Deux toponymes du Champ de Mars: ad Ciconias, ad Nixas," *Collection de l'Ecole Française de Rome* 98 (1987): 191-210. Flambard's work came to my attention since this work was written and, although neatly and ingeniously researched and argued, it has not in many particulars persuaded me. Independent of La Rocca Flambard reached the same conclusion on the Nixae as La Rocca had, but he would closely relate them to Lucina or Lucinae (see below, n. 219). I still maintain that the Nixae were where I would have them in 1978.

[110]Quilici Gigli (above, n. 109), 48ff.

[111]See *CAR* I-I 89, p. 113.

[112]Ibid., I-I 109, p. 117, that is it lay beneath Via Zanardelli/dei Soldati. Another NS path lay to the east, but whether it was a proper street is hard to say; see L. Quilici, "Un vicolo ed una torre medioevale a Tor di Nona e loro implicazioni nell'antica topografia del Campo Marzio," *Bull. Comm.* 86 (1978-79): 141-151.

[113]See below, sect. II.8.

The dedications to Silvanus found below the Via degli Acquasparta were treated by me in 1978. At that time I did not treat the nearby dedication to Silvanus Pantheus on the perhaps mistaken assumption that its shrine was not a public, but a private shrine.

Three shrines for Silvanus stood in this sector. That further west was situated by the Tarentum and its god was likened to Pan by the poet Martial. The middle one was situated near the Nixae where the October Horse was sacrificed on October 15. The third shrine lay somewhere to the east of the others and was in all likelihood also linked to the god Pan.

II.6 Silvanus Pantheus and Pan

The church of St. Augustine does not reach back so far as antiquity and, for all intents and purposes, supplants a much older church of St. Tryphon.[114] (See Plan 2, nos. 5 and 9.) It is located north of the ancient Stadium, not 80 meters east of the site of the discovery of the inscriptions of the votive games to Jupiter and the five monumental masks. In the course of time the church has come to house two inscriptions that presumably came from the vicinity.[115] The older inscription is couched in unexceptional Latin; the latter, in exceptional Greek. The one without the other would be considered a banality worthy of little notice. They belonged, I shall argue, to the same shrine but derive from quite different periods.

The Latin inscription runs: Sancto Silvano Pan/theo s(acrum). M. Fulvius Eras/tus cum suis d(ono) d(edit).[116] Silvanus Pantheus, "All-god," is met only twice besides the Roman inscription. At Spanish Italica, the *origo* of the emperor Hadrian, a freedman of his wife Sabina put up a dedication to Silvanus Pantheus for the health of that emperor and empress.[117] At High Rochester an altar was raised *ex voto* to Silvanus Pantheus for the health of a military tribune and his wife.[118] We may infer from this slight provincial evidence that at Rome Fulvius offered for the health of himself and/or his own (*sui*).

---

[114]See below, sect. II.10.

[115]*CAR* I-I, 116, p. 119. If the small marble base given to some unnamed god and found in front of St. Augustine's can be taken as index of the source of the inscriptions now in the church, the original shrine lay not 50 m. south of the doors of the church. See *CIL* VI (710 =) 31123 and *CAR* I-I, 135, p. 122. For a fine example of affirmation of the working assumption that ancient stones have not traveled far to lodge in a local church, see below, at nn. 172-174.

[116]*CIL* VI 695, apparently a tablet, reported to be set in the pavement of the chapel of S. Angelo (*non vidi*).

[117]*ILS* 3563.

[118]CIL VII 1038 = R. G. Collingwood and R. P. Wright, *The Roman Inscriptions of Britain* (Oxford 1965) no. 1271.

In Rome as elsewhere the rarely met Pantheus occurs alone.[119] In the same vein one Roman offering "to the gods and to the goddesses" was a bronze sculpture of "all-gods" in the year A.D. 157.[120] The dedication to Silvanus Pantheus was probably also made in the second century.[121]

Priapus Pantheus, attested in the Balkans in A.D. 235, would not detain us for long[122] were it not for an elaborate hymn to Priapus found in Tivoli from the same period. A dedication to the Genius of the Numen of the Powerful, Strong and Unconquerable Priapus, the poem repeats the acclamation of Priapus as father of matter who desires "to be named sire and source of the world, or is very nature (*physis*) and Pan."[123] These and other less explicit hints in the hymn point directly to Pan, the all-one and the origin of matter (*hyle*), who is identified with Silvanus, lord of matter (*silva*).[124] Priapus, herein sometimes a sylvan deity, is being conflated with a peculiar Pan. In Rome Pan, an old Greek god to whom we turn next, was thought of as a deity of good health.[125]

The other inscription from St. Augustine's is of that famous prayer to Pan that Plato composes for Socrates to close the dialogue *Phaedrus.* Addressing Pan the Beloved and "all the other gods of this place," Socrates prays, "Grant to me that I be made beautiful in my soul within and that all external possessions be in harmony with my inner man. May I consider the wise man rich and may I have such wealth as only the self-restrained (*sophron*) man can endure."[126] In publishing the text Kaibel

---

[119]Wissowa (above, n. 43), 91ff.; K. Latte, *Römische Religionsgeschichte* (Munich 1960), 334-335. See *CIL* VI 557 (= *ILS* 3996), 558, 559, (= *ILS* 1383, the reign of M. Aurelius and Verus [or Commodus]), 30793, 30793a. *La collezione epigrafica dei Musei Capitolini Tituli* 6 (1987) no. 2, found on the Via delle Botteghe Oscure at its intersection with the Via d'Aracoeli. The pantheist phenomenon was not limited to the western, Latin-speaking half of the Empire.

[120]*CIL* VI 100 = *ILS* 2076: **signum aereum pantheum**, the last word may be adjectival or genitive plural of the noun. The donor is a soldier from Brixellum in the Transpadana. On matters concerning *pantheos/on* still useful is R. Peter's entry in *Roschers Lexikon der griechischen und römischen Mythologie* vol. 3.2, cols. 1555-1557.

[121]Over 150 meters NW of St. Augustine's was found: *CIL* VI 546 (p. 535, and no. 30790), a dedication to the Numina Sancta and exhibiting Aesculapius and Hygia in relief. See *CAR* I-I, 66, p. 109. Its donor is presumably the same man who elsewhere honors Vesta and is an officer of the Association of Millers and Bakers in A.D. 144; see *CIL* VI 787 and 1002 (= *ILS* 3313, 7269). The *numina sancta*, surely a health "collective" of deities, betokened by Aesculapius and Hygia, remain as vague as "the gods and goddesses" of *CIL* VI 100; cf. VI 30685, 30983, but they suggest that deities propitious to good health as were originally Dis and Proserpina were worshipped in this zone in the middle of the second century.

[122]*CIL* III 1139 = *ILS* 3582.

[123]*CIL* XIV 3565 = *CLE* 1504; the donor, presumably a freedman of Philip the Arab was "advised by a dream." On Pan and Priapus see Brommer (below, n. 129) col. 1004.

[124]See below at nn. 135, 140-144.

[125]*IGUR* 158, a Pan for Dionysos given by her freedman for the health of Ceionia Plautia, sister of the co-emperor L. Verus (see Palmer, above, n. 107, p. 244); and *IGUR* 184, a thank-offering to the lord (*anax*) of health and daimon (i.e. to Pan) by a cured man. In my earlier article I had omitted discussion of shrines of Silvanus that seemed health associations because of their private character.

[126]Plato *Phaedrus* 279bc; the translation is that of the *LCL*.

stated that its genuineness was assured by details of its bad orthography, especially iotacism, and that it had apparently been inscribed on a decorative bust (herm) of Socrates.[127] Such a bust, carved with a legend from the *Crito*,[128] existed at Rome.

This text of Plato's *Phaedrus* bristles with "mistakes":

1. ὦ φίλε Πάν τε καὶ ἄλλοι
2. ὅσοι τῆδε θελοιητε (read θεοί, δοίητέ)
3. μοι καλῶ γενεσταε (read γενέσθαι)
4. ταδωθεν (read τἄνδοθεν) ταξωθεν (read ἔξωθεν)
5. δὲ ὅσα ἔξω τοῖς ἐντὸς
6. ειναε (read εἶναί) μοι φιλα (read φίλια) πλούσιον
7. δὲ νομιζοιμοι (read νομίζοιμι) τὸν σοφόν τὸ δὲ
8. χρυσον (read χρυσοῦ) πλῆθος εἴη μοι
9. θεον (read ὅσον) μήτε φέρειν
10. μήτε ἄγειν
11. διναετο (read δύναιτο)
12. ἄλλος
13. ἢ ὁ
14. σώφρον

Iotacism and failure to elide are forgivable. But Kaibel also looks leniently upon the text because some errors might be blamed on the copyist. Few should be attributed to him (Smetius). A reason for the text's language will be laid at another's feet.

The likelihood of mere coincidence bringing together a dedication to Silvanus Pantheus and a prayer to Pan in the same neighborhood is unthinkable because, besides the obvious Pan/Pantheus relation, Pan and Silvanus are rendered identical especially in philosophical and more especially Neo-Platonic discussion. We now turn to the development and character of this Pan, the All-god and the Lord of Matter.

The Pan of the *Phaedrus* haunted the Attic countryside at a shrine on the Ilissus along with the Nymphs, who may be the other gods Socrates invoked.[129] Plato in another dialogue seems to be the earliest to play on the name of the god in regard to the adjective *pan* 'all'.[130]

Midway in the dialogue between Phaedrus and Socrates Pan and the Nymphs in their setting on the Ilissus are declared the rhetorical betters

---

[127]Kaibel in *IG* XIV 1215.

[128]*IG* XIV 1214, quoting *Crito* 46b. Comparable busts, without quotation, are nos. 1216-1218, as well as nos. 1196-1201 (Platonic busts). For busts of literary figures see L. Moretti, "Erme acefale iscritte, edite e inedite", *Arch. Class.* 25-26 (1973-1974): 464-471.

[129]See in W. H. Roscher ed., *Ausführliches Lexikon der griechischen und römischen Mythologie*, vol. 3.1, col. 1361 and Fr. Brommer in *RE* Supplbd. 8 (1956) cols. 949-1008, esp. 993, for a summary of Pan studies.

[130]Plato *Cratylus* 408bc. Of course they have dissimilar stems and different *etyma*. See Brommer (above, n. 129) cols. 969, 1005-1006. The word play occurs for instance in Castorion's hymn on which see P. Bing, "Kastorion of Soloi's Hymn to Pan (*Supplementum Hellenisticum* 310)," *Amer. Journ. of Philology* 106 (1985): 502-509.

of Lysias whose discourse on love has just ended.[131] This rhetorical inspiration will be exemplified in the next section. The philosophy teacher of Aulus Gellius at Athens in the mid-second century A.D. remarked that the study of the *Phaedrus* was aimed at improving the eloquence of his Greek, not of his life.[132]

That the *Phaedrus* was known to the Neo-Platonist thinkers contemporary with our stone can be amply demonstrated, even if their direct attention to the prayer to Pan cannot be shown. In Rome of the fifth century the Greek dialogue was still known.[133] Even later among the Alexandrians a commentary on the *Phaedrus* was published there.[134]

The oldest attested philosophical speculation on Pan's name is found in the "Nature of the Gods" by the Roman Annaeus Cornutus who lived under Nero. Pan is all, the one and only begotten world (*cosmos*), is Priapos, guardian of gardens and vineyards.[135] When over a century later Pan is adopted by the "Orphic" theology, he is compared with Attis, "as a Bacchus, as a shepherd of the white stars."[136] To be sure, Attis was a shepherd but the white stars refer to the Neo-Platonists' Pan.

For Plotinus's disciple and biographer Porphyry, Pan has become the symbol of the All whose horns symbolize the sun and the moon and whose spotted pelt symbolizes the stars in the sky.[137]

Far more elaborate is the grand scheme articulated by Vettius Agorius Praetextatus in the first book of Macrobius's *Saturnalia*. Pan, who is called Inuus (because that is the god named in the *Aeneid* instead of Silvanus; see below), is the Sun. Arcadians call him the lord of matter

---

[131]Plato *Phaedrus* 263de. A distant Neo-Platonic echo of this conceit may be found in Iamblichus, *De Myster.* pp. 122-123 Parthey, on the inspiration of Pan and the Nymphs in respect to the excesses of body and soul!

[132]A. Gellius *NA* 1.9.8-11; cf. 2.5. His teacher was the philosopher L. Calvisius Taurus from Beirut (cf. *SIG*³ 368A, from Delphi in A.D. 163). His name is also given as Calbenus, i.e. Calvinus. (Such a name as Calvisius Calvinus would be by no means unusual). See also the Greek letter in the *corpus* of Fronto (ed. Van den Hout, 234-239) that is inspired by the *Phaedrus.*

[133]See Macr. *Sat.* 1.23.5 where *Phaedrus* (246e-247a) is quoted but is attributed to the *Timaeus* by Macrobius. This passage is found in the famous 'Neo-Platonic' speech of Vettius Agorius Praetextatus. See below.

[134]P. Coureur, ed. *Hermiae Alexandrini in Platonis* Phaedrum *scholia. Bibl. Ec. Haut. Et.* 133 (Paris 1901). Hermias has a different, but uninteresting, semantic explanation of the name Pan (265-266). His work is derived from his teacher's lectures; see Praechter, *RE* 8.1 (1912) cols. 732-735. For rhetorical and philosophical education of the period and this commentary see G. A. Kennedy, "Later Greek Philosophy and Rhetoric," *Philosophy and Rhetoric* 13 (1980): 181-197.

[135]Cornutus *Nat. Deor.* ch. 27, p. 148 Osann (see Osann, pp. 325ff. for comment). This comparison with Priapus antedates the Priapic hymn by nearly two centuries; see above at n. 124.

[136]Hippol. *Ref. Omn. Haer.* 5.9.7-9.

[137]Prophyry *peri agalmaton* 9, on p. 18* of J. Bidez, *Vie de Porphyre* (Ghent 1913, repr. Hildesheim 1964); the treatise is also cited *De imaginibus.* For the treatise and its sources see Bidez, pp. 143-157. Bidez refers to Cornutus as a source for no. 9, and elsewhere in the treatise. Pan's cave is found in Porphyry's *De antro Nympharum* 20, p. 70 Nauck. See next note.

(hyle), meaning not lord of woods *(silvae)* but the tyrant of all material substance, "whose source of matter of all bodies, be they divine or earthly, comprises being." His horns and beard show the nature of light. With passing reference to the Sun, to Pan's pipes and to Attis and to his caprine hoofs Macrobius has Vettius Agorius discourse further on the earthly elements, the entire substance, on heavenly harmony and the god Pan as the sun who is *moderator sphaerarum omnium*. There is something here for men of any belief. Formerly Porphyry's treatise on idols was thought to be the source of this Macrobian passage but now Porphyry's treatise on the Sun is given the nod.[138] If Cracco Ruggini is correct in her new interpretation of the anonymous poem *contra paganos* that Vettius Agorius Praetextatus himself drew this Christian fire and that his priesthoods and his religious fervor are being specifically pilloried we can more easily understand the polemicist's *qui c⟨unc⟩tis Faunosque deos persuaserat esse/ Egeriae Nymphae comites Satyrosque Panosque,/ Nympharum Bacchique comes Triviaeque sacerdos etc.*[139] The outright worship of Pan implicit in this polemic cannot be materially substantiated for this late date.

In addition to the literary imposition of Prophyry's influence on Vettius Agorius Praetextatus, Servius, or more justly Donatus, the commentator on Vergil's poems, was indebted to Porphyry or to some other Neo-Platonist. Beyond Cornutus, his source's base, the commentator on *Ecl.* 2.31 makes Pan the All, whose horns show likeness to the rays of the sun and the horns of the moon and whose pelt is starred in the likeness of the stars because he is the god of all nature.[140] More or less, Pan is Inuus and the god of the Lupercal and is Faunus or Fatuus *(et alii)*.[141] When Silvanus comes in for Servius's (Donatus's) full treatment he is dubbed god of matter *(theos hylikos, deus hyles)*, a matter that is the sediment of all elements *(faex omnium elementorum)*.[142] Some of these notions may have percolated from Prophyry.[143] But there were other

---

[138]Macr. *Sat* 1.22.2-7, is paraphrased in the text above. The whole passage, *Sat.* 1.17.2-23.22, was attributed by Bidez (above, n. 128), 150-151, to the *peri agalmaton* on pp. 9* and 13* (there is also similar matter on pp. 16* and 23*. P. Courcelle, *Les Lettres grecques en occident de Macrobe à Cassiodor,* 2nd ed. (Paris 1948), Engl. tr. (Cambridge MA 1969), 28-31, attributes much of the whole section on the names of the gods to Porphyry's *peri Heliou (de Sole)*; also see 45-47. That the notions are emanating principally from the Neo-Platonists around Plotinus and not from Cornutus (whose work has indirectly influenced Macr. *Sat.* 1.17), Vettius Agorius makes clear at *Sat.* 1.17.4 where he says *unde* ἓν τὸ πᾶν *sapientum principes prodiderunt.*

[139]*Cod. Par. Lat.* 8084, lines 67-74. See L. Cracco Ruggini, "Il paganesimo romano tra religione e politica (384-394 d.C.): per una reinterpretazione del *Carmen contra paganos,*" *Acc. Naz. Lincei,* Mem. Cl. Sc. Mor., Stor. Filol., ser. 8, 23 (1979), 3-141, esp. pp. 98-99.

[140]Serv. on Verg. *Ecl.* 2.31; Junius Phylarg. on 2.32 also recurs to a like explanation of *natura omnium rerum.* Isid. *Etym.* 8.11.81-83 is in part drawn from the source of Serv. on *Ecl.* 2.31; the latter part of his "definition," though unique, must come from a source that had numerological interests.

[141]Serv. on Verg. *Aen.* 1.372, 6.775, 8.343, 8.344, 8.663.

[142]Serv. on Verg. *Aen.* 8.601, cf. on *Georg.* 2.494.

[143]Cf. Courcelle (above, n. 138), 46-47.

kindred souls lurking in the learned past to bolster a faltering Vergilian commentator.[144]

From late antiquity we have then a "philosophical" portrait drawn, if not to life, at least to the likeness of a once rustic Greek deity hypostasized to Universal Matter. The Socratic prayer to Pan, excerpted from the *Phaedrus,* could have just as well adorned an image of Pan as a bust of Socrates, especially if the Pan was meant for the shrine of Silvanus Pantheus.

The state of the carved Platonic quotation permits us to think of a barely (il)literate person, speaking or writing, composing the text. It is the text of a careless man or of a man indifferent to the rules and niceties of language, a man who is the antithesis of the Lysias who is renowned in the dialogue. There is a third kind of man who might have produced the inelegant text: a man who deliberately scorned proper spelling and like rules. On the showing of his disciple and biographer Porphyry, the paramount Neo-Platonist Plotinus teaching in Rome or anywhere exhibited just such carelessness or indifference, not to say a proclivity to downright error.[145] The iotacisms of the text tell us that it was carved late enough. But the inconsistencies show something more. The very vehicle of a prayer to a god of rhetorical elegance, or at least inspiration, has been rendered inelegant by hiatus, by misspelling, by mispronunciation, in a word, by flagrant vulgarisms. The substance of the prayer is stripped, as it were, of its rhetorical veneer. To think otherwise is hazardous. Either we imagine an ignorant person wanting a quotation from Plato couched in the forms of the ignorant or we imagine a man who has read the *Phaedrus* trying to express some of its doctrine by a striking illustration of what the words should *not* be, whether written (as carved) or spoken (as copied for the carving). Here we have two *jeux,* one *d'esprit* and another *de mot.*

We have an acknowledgment of continuity between Silvanus All-god and the All-god *par excellence.* What we lack is a neutral offering to a mere Silvanus or a Pan.

Plotinus's personal views on the gods are met only in the story of his attending a kind of seance in one of Rome's temples of Isis when an Egyptian priest drew out his *daimon.*[146] Plotinus himself came from Egypt so that he could not have been a stranger to such folk-beliefs. What he might have thought of the divinity Pan is not known. His

---

[144]See the *Brevis Expositio* on Verg. *Georg* 1.17 where the mythographer Apollodorus is quoted *quoniam universum, id est* τὸ πᾶν, *huic deo sit adtributum,* with more on horns, sun, moon, pelt and stars. See Apollodorus *Bibl.* 1.4.1 in *Myth. Gr.* vol. 1, p. 11 Wagner.

[145]Porph. *Vit. Plot.* 8, 13, 19-20, 26. Toward the end of the *Phaedrus* Plato has his interlocutors discuss the relative worth of the written and spoken word (277-278b); those words, too, are germane to the expression of the carved text's language.

[146]Porph. *Vit. Plot.* ch. 10, wherein Porphyry also tells of his teacher's praeternatural power of reversing curses, and in ch. 11 of reading minds. For the incident at the Iseum see E. R. Dodds, *The Greeks and the Irrational* (Boston 1957), 283-311.

school at Rome was frequented by men of imperial prominence as well as by lesser lights from the Orient.[147] On Porphyry's telling the imperial couple, Gallienus and Salonina, fostered the school of Plotinus and would have refounded in Campania a philosophers' colony to be named Platonopolis, had not the envy of courtiers forestalled them.[148] Gallienus and Salonina perhaps advanced the interests of the "school" but Porphyry acknowledges only the one disappointment. Porphyry himself had at least one disciple of senatorial rank.[149]

Plotinus's long residence and instruction in Rome, the prominence of some of his auditors, and the imperial patronage permit us to assume that the Neo-Platonist and his views were widely known in the city. Many and prosperous followers could have commissioned the inscription of the prayer to Pan. But so, too, could have the Master himself. Its inscription as we read it today betokens Plotinus's linguistic habits. If the text came from Plotinus or one of his listeners, it is the one palpable remnant of his Neo-Platonism on the soil of Rome.

The inscription will have been set beside dedications to Silvanus Pantheus. Silvanus enjoyed a theology laden with interpretation of the root *silva* =ὕλη and, by equation with Pan, of the Greek god's name as symbol of "universal matter."

---

[147]Drawing on Porph. *Vit. Plot.* chs. 2,3,7,9–11, and 20 we can get some idea of his following, both male and female. Prominent disciples included Amelius Gentilianus of Etruria who traveled to Apamaea and adopted a man of that town in Rome named Hostilianus Hesychius; at Rome Amelius became a sort of religious fanatic, especially at the time of the new moon (chs. 2,3,7,10). Castricius Firmus, evidently from near Minturnae, had pursued a public career (chs. 2,7; *PIR²* C 543). His Campanian land was acquired by the Arab Zethus, a physician (chs. 2 and 7). Three Roman senators are counted among Plotinus's sectarians: Marcellus Orrontius (read Arruntius in ch. 7); see E, Groag and A. Stein, *Prosopographia imperii Romani* (Berlin 1933-) A 1144 and Marcellus; G. Barbieri, *L'albo senatorio da Settimio Severo a Carino (193-285)* = *Studi pubblicati dall'Istituto Italiano per la Storia Antica*, fasc. 6 (Rome 1952), no. 1151. The consul of the year A.D. 266 was Sabinillus, identified tentatively as his follower of that name (ch. 7; see Barbieri, no. 1718 and Nagl *RE* 1A2.2 (1920) col. 1588); and finally Rogatianus who resigned his praetorship out of a sense of philosophy when the lictors were at his door (ch. 7; see Barbieri, no. 1713 and cf. nos. 1612 and 1617). Other followers were the Alexandrian physician Eustochius, the critic and poet Zoticus, the rhetor and later banker Serapion also of Alexandria, the painter Carterius (chs. 7 and 20) and assorted women and youths (chs. 9 and 11). Other than Porphyry none has made a mark.

[148]Porph. *Vit. Plot.* 12, who also says that is was supposed to perpetuate a ruined city of philosophers in Campania. Such a "colony" is otherwise unknown though it may have been mistakenly inferred from an incident in the life of Plato as reported by Diogenes Laertius, *Vit. Plat.* 3.21, where Dionysius of Syracuse reneges on a commitment to provide Plato land to "found" his Republic. Plato himself seems to have known Italiotes at first hand (see *Epist.* 7.326b-d) and is said to have visited Italy ([Plato] *Epist.* 11 and Apul. *Plat. Dogm.* 3-4). In the late second century B.C. the homegrown Campanian philosopher, Blossius of Cumae, fled the troubles following on the Gracchan debacle and assisted Aristonicus of Asia in founding the philosophically inspired Heliopolis; see Klebs *RE* 3.1 (1897) col. 571. By the third century A.D. such stories may have been blurred and conflated so as to promote the fiction of a 'philosophopolis' in Campania.

[149]His name was Chrysaorios (cf. *CIL* VI 32167 and 32186). On him and other Roman followers of Porphyry see Bidez (above n. 137), 104.

The appearance of Silvanus Pantheus, probably in the second half of the second century, of Pan in a Platonic prayer, in the following century, injects an odd note into a discussion of the discoveries in this quarter. However, we shall see that they are not phenomena in isolation from their surroundings. Underlying the quotation of Plato's *Phaedrus* is allusion to generations of teaching rhetorical elegance. Rhetorical excellence had been honored in the vicinity in the reign of Septimius Severus when Plotinus was yet a child.

II.7 To a Very Great Orator

If we seek a beneficiary of the blessings bestowed on a public speaker by some divinity we have no distance to go. In the Piazza S. Apollinare where the two consular inscriptions of the votive games to Jupiter for the return of Augustus in 13 and 7 B.C. and the five monumental masks were uncovered, two statue bases dedicated to C. Sallius Aristaenetus were found in front of the church porch. (See Plan 2, no. 7). Nearly identical texts, doubtless drafted in common, were inscribed by the donor peoples of Asculum Picenum and Ancona (also in Picenum) for this senator who was honored for his *humanitas* and his *abstinentia*. He had been a judge in Picenum when the two communities would have experienced his virtues. Other magistracies, offices and priesthoods were noted. After listing his public appointments the townsmen wrote *oratori maximo . . . propter humanitatem abstinentiam*.[150] The recipient of this accolade is thought to be Aristaenetus the "sophist" of Byzantium who had been a disciple of Chrestos of the same city.[151] In that case, Sallius Aristaenetus will have flourished in the early third century under the Severans. The virtues the men of Asculum and Ancona applauded could have been narrowly understood as the virtues of a good *iuridicus,* but they are also what Socrates prayed for in his prayer to Pan, to the Pan who could inspire the oratory of Lysias. The *humanitas* of the Romans rendered the Greek idea of *philanthropia*.[152] The senator's *abstinentia* recalls the *sophron* of the Platonic prayer.[153] Nevertheless, an

---

[150]*CIL* VI 1511(= *ILS* 2934), 1512; see *CAR* I-I, 114, p. 118. The texts do not yield a clue as to his dates.

[151]Philostratus *Vit. Soph.* 2.11 (591); see Nagl, *RE* 1A2 (1920) cols. 1908-1910.

[152]See J. H. Oliver on Aelius Aristides's *Roman Oration* ch. 66 in J. H. Oliver, *The Ruling Power: A study of the Roman Empire in the second century after Christ through the Roman Oration of Aelius Aristides. Trans. Amer. Philos. Soc.* n. s.43.4 (1953): 930. See *TLL, s.v.* humanitas, cols. 3079-3082.

[153]The honors from the townsmen of Ancona also mention his *efficacia*. None of these virtues is otherwise acknowledged so early and so publicly at Rome by inscription. Both *abstinentia* and *humanitas* are well attested virtues of statesmen before the days of Aristaenetus but *efficacia* is far rarer. What wants emphasis is the era in which these compliments were publicly paid. Two centuries later they would have become banal.

emphasis on Sallius Aristaenetus as a very great orator is surprising because so unusual.[154]

Since the two inscriptions now in St. Augustine's cannot be considered *in situ,* we may or may not link them directly to the honorific text of the two statue bases. Yet the extraordinary element in the inscriptions for Aristaenetus's statue base reflects both the text and context of the prayer to Pan. How Silvanus Pantheus may have served in this cause cannot be known.

As I have reconstructed circumstances of the dedication of the inscribed prayer to Pan, it would have been erected during Plotinus's sojourn at Rome ca. A.D. 244-270,[155] or under his continuing influence. Therefore, Pan's appearance has been anticipated by the accolade for Sallius Aristaenetus. The honors for Aristaenetus suggest that the inscription of the Platonic prayer and its dedication conformed to circumstances already prevailing at the time of Plotinus's birth.

A kind of continuity of literary interests haunts this sector: five monumental theatrical masks of marble found with records of votive games, an inscription of a prayer to Pan composed by a great philosopher and quoted by a "vulgarian," a pair of dedications to a "very great orator" from Byzantium.

By varying accounts beside or beneath St. Augustine's lay a large building described in Renaissance Latin as *ingens quaedam testudo subterranea,* seen and described as covered with many large blocks of fallen buildings.[156]

Here we presumably have a building of unusual shape. With some hesitation I propose to identify it as Hadrian's Athenaeum whose whereabouts are quite unknown. Overcome with awe for things Greek Hadrian went so far as to introduce the Eleusinian mysteries of Demeter and Kore to Rome and to found a school of the liberal arts (*ludus*

---

[154]From the computerized index of CIL VI.7 it appears that no other man of the early principate was honored as an *orator maximus;* comparable compliments belong to a later age. The first comparable accolade I find is that by T. Fl. Postumius Varus, evidently the urban prefect in A.D. 271, for his grandfather whom he describes as *orator utraque facundia maximus* (*CIL* VI 1416 = *ILS* 2929) and the grandson himself is called *orator* on his tombstone (*CIL* VI 1417 = *ILS* 2940). Another grandson of the same man is also called *orator* and like his kinsman claimed to be a "follower" (*sectator*) of the grandfather (*CIL* VI 1418 = *ILS* 2941). The orator, very great in both literatures, was M. Postumius Festus, otherwise known as a contemporary of Cornelius Fronto; see Lambertz, *RE* 22.1 (1953) cols. 950-952.

[155]The dates are firmly set by Porphyry; see H.-R. Schwyzer, *RE* 21.2 (1951) cols. 473-474. T. D. Barnes, "The Chronology of Plotinus' Life," *Greek, Roman and Byzantine Studies* 17 (1976): 65-70

[156]R. Lanciani, *Storia degli Scavi* (above, n. 10) 1, p. 81 and 4, p. 77. On his *Forma Vrbis Romae* (Milan 1893-1907) pl. 15, he has made plural the reported *testudo* and charted *testudines ingentes* immediately west of St. Augustine's and south of St. Tryphon's. The entry of *CAR* I-I, 116, p. 119, makes the remains lie beneath St. Augustine's and says, "grande volta sotterranea coperta da ruderi." If it was "subterranean" in antiquity it would have been periodically filled with flood waters.

ingenuarum artium) of the kind called an Athenaeum.[157] At the time of Marcus Aurelius and Commodus the most distinguished Greek professor held forth in the Athenaeum, to which senators and knights flocked to hear his rhetorical displays.[158] In A.D. 193 the consul summoned the senate to the fateful meeting at which Didius Julianus was deposed and Septimius Severus hailed emperor. The Athenaeum, "called after the fact of its educational purpose," hosted the meeting which Dio Cassius himself attended.[159] From the *Historia Augusta* we learn of recitals by poets and rhetors or debates (*controversiae*) declaimed in the imperial presence at the Athenaeum.[160] In the second half of the fifth century Sidonius Apollinaris could contrast *Athenaeum* with *monasterium,* the one a place of quiet and the other a setting of uproar in the quaking seats of its wedgeshaped theater sections (*cunei*).[161] From his description of the hall of the Athenaeum we may infer a roofed structure with a sloping and semicircular chamber whose "pit" held the podium of the teacher or speaker or recitalist. Whether the ruins of a building with an altitude and plan conformable to *cunei* might be called in the Renaissance a *testudo,* I cannot affirm.

At Rome the oldest attested "hall of fame" for public speakers will be that established in or by the Palatine libraries of the temple of Apollo. There Tiberius's nephew and adopted son Germanicus was accorded a statue among the masters of eloquence at his death.[162] The Severan dedications to Sallius Aristaenetus as a very great orator, commendable for his *humanitas* and *abstinentia* are not, in a way, unprecedented. Surely an appropriate place for honoring a Byzantine *rhetor* would have been the Athenaeum, planned for and frequented by students of Greek letters. As a public lecture hall the Athenaeum could have been available to the likes of Plotinus whom the imperial couple patronized and senators heard.

In section II.2 I suggested that it was in proximity to the site of two votive games for his return that Augustus set up a very costly compital statue of Jupiter the Tragic Player. In that vein Augustus, too, may have

---

[157]Aur. Vict. *Caes.* 14.3.

[158]Philostratus *Vit. Soph.* 2.10 (589). The rhetor was Hadrian of Tyre. Philostratus might be taken to imply that students of Latin letters normally did not attend the Athenaeum; surely he implies that they did not normally attend the lectures of the Greek professor. The *HA Alex.* 35 contradicts such an implication.

[159]Dio Cass. 74.17.3-4, wishing to tell his readers that the building was not a temple of Athena, or the Chalcidicum of the Senate (51.22.1). For recent discussion of the Athenaeum see Chr. Callmer, "Athenaeum," *Opusc. Rom.* 7 (1969), 277-284, whom I cannot follow, and A. Fraschetti, "*L'Atrium Minervae* in epoca tardantica," *Opusc. Inst. Rom. Finl.* 1 (1981), 27-28, who firmly rejects any identity of the senate building (Chalcidicum and Atrium Minervae) at the Forum with Hadrian's Athenaeum.

[160]*HA Pert.* 11.3, *Alex.* 35, *Gord.* 3.4, Valueless indications, I believe.

[161]Sid. Apoll. *Epist.* 2.9.4, 4.8.5, 9.9.13, 9.14.2. Sidonius knew Rome well since he was urban prefect in 468 and had served there even earlier. See Schanz-Hosius-Krüger, *Geschichte der römischen Litteratur* 4.2 (Munich 1920), 43-55.

[162]The texts are the Tabula Hebana and Tac. *Ann.* 2.83. See S. Weinstock, "The Image and the Chair of Germanicus," *Journal of Roman Studies* 47 (1957): 144-155.

begun to promote the liberal arts practiced here. Public land left open for certain kinds of periodic festivals may have been appropriated by Hadrian for the building of his Athenaeum. My hypothesis for situating the school of liberal arts where strangely described ruins are once reported rests upon the choice for honoring Aristaenetus with two statues in this quarter and the choice of installing an inscription of the Platonic prayer from the closing of the *Phaedrus*.

II.8. The Foundation of a Forum

In the fourth and fifth centuries at least five forums were "founded." They present themselves to us as a kind of curiosity, for they can have been forums like no other earlier forum. All five can be relatively dated and two can be absolutely dated. One of them was established not 50 meters west of where the statues of Sallius Aristaenetus stood. Since, however, I know no study, convenient or otherwise, of this phenomenon, I shall review the evidence of this forum building while reserving the best attested and most pertinent to last.

In chronological order the forums are those established by an Apronianus, probably the urban prefect of A.D. 362-364, by Eupraxius urban prefect of 374, by Acilius Glabrio Sibidius Spedius early in the fifth century, by Petronius Maximus, twice urban prefect and briefly emperor, between 443 and 445, and by Epityncanus as urban prefect in 450.[163]

On 24 January 400 the emperors addressed the urban prefect on the subject of a fraud and the privileges of shippers (*navicularii*). Their decision was posted at Rome in the Forum of Apronianus.[164] Of the known Aproniani of the era only one seems a likely candidate for founding the forum.[165] The urban prefect in the years 362-364 L. Turcius Apronianus Asterius enjoys the reputation of a renowned administrator and builder who tried to improve the distribution of meat in the city.[166] Since

[163]Because of an apparent tie between the urban prefecture and forum building A. Chastagnol, *La préfecture urbaine à Rome sous le Bas-empire* (Paris, 1960), 356-357, gives a scant glance at the subject. Also scant is the footnote of B. Ward-Perkins, *From Classical Antiquity to the Middle Ages* (Oxford 1984), 45 n. 33, who mistakenly believes that these forums had existed earlier than the evidence of their "foundation."

[164]*Cod. Theod.* 13.5.29. All of 13.5 concerns the *navicularii* whose chief responsibility was the food supply (*annona*); see 13.5.2-3, 9, 27 (on a third part of the urban "canon" see below), and 38. The Forum Aproniani is listed as one of the fourteen forums of the City by Polemius Silvius.

[165]In A. H. M. Jones et al., *Prosopography of the Later Roman Empire* vol. 1 (Cambridge 1971) there are ten Aproniani but only nos. 9 and 10 were urban prefects. I am discussing no. 10.

[166]*Cod. Theod.* 14.4.3 is addressed to him. All of 14.4 concerns "de suariis, pecuariis et susceptoribus vini ceterisque corporatis". (In 14.4.4 the imperial decision is carved on bronze and posted at Rome in the Forum Suarium.) See Apronianus's edicts on the sale

the Forum Suarium held the activities of the *canon suarius* and the temple of the Sun, those of the *canon vinarius,* we might infer from the content of the imperial letter of 400 and from the name Forum Aproniani that the urban prefect of 362–364 founded a forum for the corporate and business activities of the shippers (*navicularii*) who served Rome.[167]

Very likely in 374 A.D. the three emperors gave, at least nominally, a forum to the Roman people whose construction was undertaken by the urban prefect Eupraxius. The inscription recording the imperial munificence is reported by the "Einsiedln pilgrim" as standing in the Forum Palatinum,[168] a name he probably did not read on the spot. Although its precise locality is not attested, it is well to bear in mind that the Palatine temple of Apollo had burned to the ground in March of A.D. 363[169] and was doubtless not rebuilt. The next forum to be treated seems to have supplanted ruins. Therefore, the forum of Eupraxius may have been laid out on the ruins of Apollo's temple.

Petronius Maximus boasted so much that he came to an untimely end as a usurping emperor. On the two epigraphic texts recording a new forum he reminded his public of his four (two urban and two praetorian) prefectures and two ordinary consulships. Although he dedicated the new forum to the master of human affairs, the emperor Valentinianus, who had been the source of his many honors, he claimed that he founded the forum (*fori conditor*) after he had cleared the debris (*squalore summoto*). Evidently the forum was situated on the street beneath the Via Labicana, near the baths of Titus and in the vicinity of St. Clement's.[170] No forum of any sort had stood here before. On the other hand, we know that in 442, the nearby Amphitheater had been

---

of mutton (*CIL* VI 1770) and pork (1771). The former was found near St. Peter in Chains, the site of the urban prefecture; the latter mentions the *levamen ex titulo canonico vinario* accorded to the pork-butchers. See Chastagnol (above, n. 163), 326–330, on these edicts and on the *canon suarius* and *canon vinarius.*

[167]Their corporation is attested by *CIL* VI 1022 = 31228, 1674, 1639, 1740. The last is one of several honorific bases for Memmius Vitrasius Orfitus (*PLRE* 1, Orfitus 3, urban prefect 353–355, 357–359); the pertinent donors are *corpus naviculariorum, corpus pistorum magnariorum et castrensariorum,* and *antiquissimum corpus susceptorum Ostiensium sive Portuensium.* Ammianus (27.3.2–3) refers to the *navicularii,* to a case of fraud and thereupon incidentally mentions the urban prefect Apronianus. On the shippers and the *canon frumentarius* see Chastagnol (above, n. 163), 301–308; on *susceptores* cf. above, n. 166.

[168]*CIL* VI 1177 = *ILS* 776: curante Flavio Eupraxi[o] v(iro) c(larissimo) [praef(ecto) urbi]. See *PLRE* 1, Eupraxius.

[169]*Amm. Marc.* 23.3.3.

[170]*CIL* VI 1197, 1198 = *ILS* 807/8, variously reported. See *PLRE* 2, Maximus 22. From his titles the period of 443 to 445 is estimated for the building of the forum. S. Panciera has brought to my attention an inscribed architrave, reused in the rebuilding of St. Peter's, that may have come from this forum: ornatum Petronius Max[imus. See B. M. Apollonj Ghetti *et. al., Esplorazioni sotto la confessione di San Pietro in Vaticano* 2 vols. (Vatican City 1951), 185 (from the photograph of Tav. LXXVI, I would read o/rnatum Petronius M[aximus). The participle should modify *forum.* See G. Lugli, *I monumenti antichi di Roma e suburbio,* vol. 3 ('A traverso le regioni') (Rome 1938), 387–388.

damaged by an earthquake.[171] Perhaps a collapsed building was re-
moved to provide a forum. On the other hand, the forum may have
served as an excuse for not rebuilding what had collapsed.

In the church of St. Vitus stood a base that read: Fl. Eurycles Epityncanus u(ir) c(larissimus), praef(ectus) urb(i), conditor huius fori,
curavit. The base was being reused in 450, the year of Epityncanus's
prefecture, and had formerly belonged to an object set up on 23 January 243: coll(ocatum) X k(alendas) Febr(uarias) Arriano et Papo cos.[172]
The day fell three days after the birthday of one of the emperors Gordian.[173] Since Gordian I and II ruled so briefly, probably only the birthday of Gordian III has entered the calendar. The year A.D. 243 falls in
Gordian III's reign. This base may well have once held his statue in
honor of his birthday. The same text of this *conditor huius fori* was inscribed on another base found *in situ* very near the Arch of Gallienus
where St. Vitus's church still stands.[174] For no good reason these texts
are referred to the Forum Esquilinum that lay somewhere in the vicinity of the arch which was in truth the Porta Esquilina.[175] The text,
perhaps marking statues of Epityncanus himself, emphasizes his foundation of the forum just as Petronius Maximus had done a few years
earlier.

The earliest assertion of the "founding" of these late forums was
made in the case of the third oldest in the series to which we now turn.

The bases that praised the very great orator Aristaenetus for his re-
straint and culture stood 50 meters east of a forum later founded sometime in the first quarter of the fifth century. It stood by an ancient street
that was perhaps the only NS street leading to the Tiber and that lay
parallel to the NS streets leading to the Pons Aelius and the street
beneath the Via della Scrofa.[176] With the discovery of the ancient street
came the fragment of a base set up by the same man already known to
have placed two other bases with comparable texts. Since the two other
bases had belonged in the collection of Cardinal Altemps whose residence stood (and stands) beside the site of the new discovery we have
ascertained the original provenience of the two better known texts.[177]

---

[171]Paul. Diac. *Hist. Rom.* 13.16.
[172]*CIL* VI 1662 = *ILS* 5357. See *PLRE* 2, Epityncanus.
[173]Degrassi (above, n. 2), 402.
[174]*CIL* VI 31888.
[175]See Platner-Ashby, *TDAR*, pp. 224-225, 407; Lugli (above, n. 14) vol. 3, pp. 131-132.
Lugli (above, n. 170) pp. 418-419, makes the Macellum Liviae a part of this Forum
Esquilinum, but that seems impossible since the Market of Livia was refurbished in A.D.
375 (*CIL* VI 1178 = *ILS* 5592). Indeed the very sites of the forum and the *macellum* are
matters of dispute, recently compounded. See R. E. A. Palmer, "Customs on Market
Goods Imported into the City of Rome," *The Seaborne Commerce of Ancient Rome: Studies in
Archaeology and History = Memoirs of the American Academy in Rome* 36 (1980): 228, n. 29.
[176]*NdSc* 1904, p. 401. The street in question lay under the Via dei Soldati/Zanardelli.
See *CAR* I-I, 109. p. 117, above n. 112.
[177]The text found by the street paving is *CIL* VI 37119 = *ILS* 8986 (twice in *CAR* I-I as
nos. 109 and 112, pp. 117-118) and its subject was the maternal great-great-grandfather

(See Plan 2, no. 6.) In all cases the donor of the bases and their statues styles himself outfitter of (this) place, *loci ornator.* The man descends from a noble family that could trace its prominence back to the third century B.C.[178] Our only firm date is known by the fact that Anicius Acilius Glabrio Faustus, three times an urban prefect, dedicated the statue of his father-in-law when he served as consul in A.D. 438.[179] The donor's father had "founded" the forum. Here is the text honoring the father:

> Spedii (*sc.* statua)
> Acilio Glabrioni Sibidio v(iro) c(larissimo) et omnibus
> meritis inlustri legato in provincia Achaia,
> consulari Campaniae, vicario per Gallias
> 5 septem provinciarum, sacri auditorii cogni-
> tori, fori huiusce inventori et conditori pri-
> mo, patri reverentissimo, Anicius Acilius
> Glabrio Faustus v(ir) c(larissimus), loci ornator, togatam
> statuam offerens piae non minus quam de-
> 10 votae mentis religione ponendam
> erigendamque curavit.[180]

Sibidius Spedius "discovered" and founded first this forum which the son calls the place he is outfitting by looking after the emplacement and erection of a togate statue that he offers with the respect of a dutiful and no less devoted mind. The very redundancy of addressing his most venerable father *fori huiusce inventori et conditori primo* suggests that others who founded forums before Acilius Glabrio Sibidius Spedius had claimed a foundation when they had merely refurbished. The career of Sibidius Spedius as recorded by the son indicates no urban function or official capacity in which he might have founded the forum. In the two earlier cases of Apronianus and Eupraxius the urban praefecture is assumed and restored because in the two later cases of Petronius Maximus and Epityncanus they were administering that prefecture. Furthermore the donor, Anicius Acilius Glabrio Faustus, in no case cites his own office or function as the *ornator,* but in the one, the following instance, he has added his rank, to mark the occasion of the dedication.

Here follows the honorific text of Faustus's father-in-law:

> Tarruteni (*sc.* statua)
> Tarrutenio Maximiliano v(iro) c(larissimo)

---

of the donor. The base of the statue of the donor's father is VI 1678 = *ILS* 1281; and of the donor's father-in-law is VI 1767 = *ILS* 1282. Both were owned by Card. Altemps. See below, n. 181.

[178]Man. Acilius Glabrio was the first of his family to be elected consul in 191 B.C. A descendant, twice consul and imperial candidate, claimed descent from Venus and Aeneas (Herodian 2.3.4).

[179]*PLRE* 2, Faustus 8, urban prefect between 408 and 425, in 425 and between 425 and 437. His father-in-law is *PLRE* 2, Maximilianus 3 and his father is *PLRE* 1, Sibidius.

[180]*CIL* VI 1678 = *ILS* 1281.

eloquentissimoque, consulari
Piceni anno aetatis nonodecimo,
5   vicario urbis Romae, legato amplis-
simi senatus secundo, socero
exoptatissimo, Anicius Acilius
Glabrio Faustus v(ir) c(larissimus), loci huius
ornator, togatam statuam
10 libens optuli.

The base had formerly been dedicated to a divinity. Just as there is a sacred ewer carved on this new epigraphic face there stands on the new reverse side of the base the original dedication to a goddess below which is carved

Anicius Acilius Glabrio Faustus.
v(ir) c(larissimus) consul dicavit.[181]

For his maternal forebear Faustus composed a similar honorific text that is now fragmentary and damaged, but found in situ:

[——pro dignitate]
tanti ordinis [——loci] eius [ornator togatam]
statuam proa[vi——ob] ins[igni]a ad [memoriam pos]-

---

[181]*CIL* VI 1767 = 31926 = *ILS* 1282, was re-used by Anicius Acilius Glabrio Faustus who dated the base to his consulship in 438. The base had formerly held a statue of a goddess whose name, but not epithets, was erased. At 31926 it is suggested that the base stood in Faustus's house (*domus palmata*) in the Forum near the Senate. Faustus's house *ad Palmam* (*Gesta Cod. Theod.*) is probably not that *ad Palmam* by the Senate in the sixth century; see Platner-Ashby, *TDAR*, pp. 187, 382, 604-605. At all events Faustus calls the house *his* house, not a public house. The provenience of the inscribed base VI 1767 remains a puzzle. Silvio Panciera counsels the author against assigning the base for Faustus's father-in-law to the forum founded by Sibidius. In addition to the clue supplied by the text *loci ornator, togatam statuam* which conforms both to the actual text of VI 1678 and to the restored text of VI 37119 (see below), the two bases (1678 and 1767) were reported in the collection of Card. Altemps (d. 1595), in the gardens of Montalto (also Peretti), and so forth. Prof. Panciera draws attention to the fact that Pignaria reports the discovery of VI 1767 in the Campo Vaccino, i.e. the Forum Romanum. (Hence the attempt to link it to the house of Faustus or to the *domus palmata*.) Indeed, merely on the basis of that report one would assign VI 1678, without a provenience, to the same locality. But the recent discovery of VI 37119 at the Via dei Soldati calls into question the provenience of VI 1767 precisely because the palace of Card. Altemps stands close by the find-site of VI 37119. If we allow the correctness of Pignaria's report, then we must allow at the same time that all three texts, VI 1678, 1767, and 37119, still refer to the same *locus* as the destination intended when Faustus assumed responsibility for outfitting his father's forum. (Entirely out of the question is any idea that Sibidius, bereft of urban office, "founded" the Forum Romanum.) If we allow that the destination was one and the same for all three bases, then VI 1767 was either never installed there or was transported thence. If the last situation is granted, then we are left with the following history. Card. Altemps owned VI 1678 because it was found by his palace near which VI 37119 was found over three centuries later; when VI 1767 was found in the Campo Vaccino, the same cardinal acquired it so as to own a matched pair of inscriptions from the same man for the same place (*locus*). A puzzle!

teritatis Anici[us Aci]lius Glabrio Fau[st]us v(ir)
    c(larissimus)
proavo suo ma[terno pr]o cultu reverentiae [debitae]
    [er]exit.[182]

No doubt attaches to the claim of originality of this new forum. Two generations, father and son, founded and outfitted the forum. The father apparently had no official warrant for the foundation or the son for the decoration, although he chose to dedicate at least one of the statues in the year when he could call himself consul.[183] The renowned lineage he boasted was perpetuated by his consular sons.[184]

So far as we know neither the predecessors, Apronianus and Eupraxius, nor the successors, Petronius Maximus and Epityncanus, created a kind of hall of family fame in the forums they founded. Our three statue bases are so far a unique dossier.[185] Independent testimony suggests that the forum of the Anicii Acilii was constructed for private purposes. In that case we have here an example of private enterprise unlike the public enterprise presumed in the building of the other forums. In one instance probably and in another certainly some *conditores* owned what they founded.[186]

It was the repeated and cherished view of Lanciani that beneath the church of S. Apollinaris (see Plan 2, no. 8.) lay the *statio rationis marmorum* which office somehow or other managed or superintended the

---

[182]*CIL* VI 37119 = *ILS* 8986. Dessau restored *memoriam pos[teritatis* (cf. VI 1768 *ad memoriam perpetui nominis*, 1727 *ad posteritatis memoriam*), *ma[terno*, and [*debitae*?. Palmer restores in a senatorial context *pro dignitate] tanti ordinis* (cf. VI 1698), *loci] eius [ornator togatam* after the base's two mates although the maternal great-great-grandfather might have deserved a statue differently garbed (that is, not *habitu civili*, as it would have been said in former times), and *ob] ins[igni]a* which fits exactly the gap although comparable formulas are usually fuller (e.g. VI 1736 *ob insignia eius in rem publicam merita*, X 3860 *ob insignia eius unihersa;* and cf. VI 1679 *trini magistratus insignia* and 1777 *insignia constitui locarique curavit*). Besides the *patri reverentissimo* in the honorific text for Faustus's father compare *parenti reverendo* (VI 1777) for the *reverentiae* of this text. A good example of *cultus reverentiae* is provided by the text of *CIL* VI 1679 = *ILS* 1262. For examples of a statue *habitu civili* see *CIL* VI 1549, for *armata statua* 1377, and for several kinds including *loricata statua* see 1599.

[183]We know that Faustus also rebuilt old public buildings when he was urban prefect; see *CIL* VI 1676 and 1677.

[184]See above, n. 178; his one son became consul in 483 (*PLRE* 2, Faustus 4) and another in 488 when he was urban prefect II (*PLRE* 2, Sividius, who is identified only as a descendant of Sibidius Spedius).

[185]There is no dearth of examples where one man or several men of the same family are honored by a statuary cluster (see, e.g., above, n. 167) but these examples are concentrated at the sites of their presumed mansions, and in a private setting.

[186]For a *conditor balnearum* and a *loci dominus conditorque* see P. Sabbatini Tumolesi, "Aproposito di *CIL* VI, 31917 da Praeneste (?)", *Bull. Comm.* 89 (1984) pp. 29–34, esp. p.33, n. 7 where she cites I. Iacopi in *Bolletino d'Arte* 6 (1880) pp. 15ff, which I have not seen. The "owner and founder of the place," at the head of the Via Cavour, dedicated there a statue of Jupiter Best and Greatest (*ibid.*) Again, I am in Prof. Panciera's debt. Ammianus 27.3.7 supplies a splendid example of the distinction between *instaurator* and *conditor*, the force of *exornare*, and one urban prefect's (Lampadius) boastfulness in the context of restoring what he claimed to have founded.

many marble carvers who have left their unfinished columns and statues (especially of "Trajanic" Dacians) as well as unshaped stone blocks scattered far and wide in the quarter we have been discussing.[187] From the charting of the remains it would seem that an extensive area was partially given over to "task work" in marble. Yet if such labor had been organized on a concentrated systematic scale, it has left no sign. What is more, a quarter lodging solely marbleworkers hardly seems a likely source for a Platonic dedication or a likely setting for honoring a fine public speaker from Byzantium.

Slightly to the north and west of this supposed center of marble working were put up the two dedications to Silvanus of which one was dedicated on the Ides of October, the feast of the October Horse.[188] From the moment when a tablet recorded the votive games to Jupiter for the return of Augustus in 13 B.C. down to the later third century, we meet signs of only partial occupation and diverse traces of men with literary tastes. Open spaces, might serve as an occasional site for racing chariots, for equestrian acrobats, for staging plays, not often but sometimes. Subject to flood, the land might also serve the Imperial Patrimony as a stage for working and distributing marbles. They do not float in flood. Also it is hard to imagine a Tiber flood doing much damage to a lead works. In contrast, of course, an Athenaeum would not have been well situated hereabouts. By the reign of Honorius we have no high expectations of imperial distribution of marbles for construction in the city. The nobleman Sibidius Spedius created a forum presumably on land no longer used for whatever purpose it had served earlier. I suggested above in the case of the so-called Palatine Forum that its creation may have covered the site of the temple (and *area*) of Apollo that had burned to the ground eleven years earlier.

Official abandonment of the old modes of Roman religion and the concrete structures housing its cults and ceremonies naturally permit conjecture that any considerable building in the era of state promotion of Christianity might be concealment of destroyed or obsolete centers of pagan belief. For instance, the horse sacrifice on 15 October was still being observed in the mid-fourth century. But the two other Martial chariot races had evidently disappeared.[189] At all events, the forum and

---

[187]R. Lanciani, *Bull. Comm.* 1891, pp. 18-36; *Storia degli Scavi* (above, n. 10) 1.81, 4.77; *The Ruins and Excavations of Ancient Rome* (Boston and New York, 1897), 525-527, where after the discovery of the mole at Tor di Nona he tied its dock to the traffic in the marbles of the emperors. The datable remnants under the church of S. Apollinare proved to be one lead pipe signed merely *statio patrimonii* and a column of portasanta, both from the Antonine period; see *CAR* I-I, 115, pp. 118-119, 123, p. 120. Also see R. Lanciani's *Forma vrbis Romae*, pl. 15. There is no certain and compelling proof of the nature of the building beneath St. Apollinaris.

[188]See above, sect. II.5. These dedications were about 125 m. from the site of the forum of Sibidius Spedius.

[189]It is the calendar of Filocalus that has the notice *equus ad Nixas fit;* see Degrassi (above, n.2), 521. *Fit* means 'is sacrificed'. Both the Equirria are absent from this calen-

its statues of kinsmen cannot have been too large, for the church of St. Apollinaris is said to overlie directly an ancient building. Yet the probability remains that the new forum, for all its private appearances, was laid out on public land no longer used for its onetime purpose.[190] The forum founded by Acilius Glabrio Sibidius Spedius may have been the latest, but not the last, act of encroachment upon what remained of the Trigarium and the Campus Martius (in its limited sense).

Faustus adorned his father's creation with togate statues of forebears reaching back several generations. But the installation of tokens of ancestral glory should not diminish the fact that a *forum* was still a place of business. Witness the posting of an imperial edict in the Forum Aproniani in A.D. 400 because of its apt content. The Anicii Acilii Glabriones Fausti apparently promoted their business enterprises as well as their ancestral renown.

We know that the wine traffic still flourished somewhere in this sector.

II.9 The Storks

In the edited text of the regionary gazetteers of Region IX, *Ciconias* 'Storks' is distinguished from the following item, *Nixas*. The pair follows upon *Trigarium*.[191] Just as the Nixae is met individually in the mid fourth century calendar of Filocalus who assigns the sacrifice of the October Horse *ad Nixas*,[192] the Ciconiae is met individually in the only other source to mention this locality.

An inscription, concerning fees or payment for employees in the distribution of the wines taken as tax, twice cites the place 'Ciconiae.' The inscription of wages by the piece mentions the *falancarii qui de Ciconiis ad Templum cupas referre consueverunt* and the *professionarii de Ciconiis*

---

dar: Equirria I on 27 February has been supplanted by Constantine's birthday and Equirria II on 14 March by the Mamuralia whatever they were; see Degrassi (above, n.2), 416–417, 422. Although it has no immediate bearing on rites at Rome the liturgical text of A.D. 387, the Feriale Campanum, exhibits omission of ceremonies calling for sacrifice or attendance at pagan places of worship, see Degrassi, p. 282. The Theodosian Code also contains evidence of restraints imposed on the practice of the old religion; see esp. *Cod. Theod.* 2.8 (*de feriis*) and 16.10 (*de paganis, sacrificiis et templis*), 3 in A.D. 346 on partial retention of *ludi, circenses* and *agones*, 5 in A.D. 353 on abolition of nocturnal sacrifice, and 10 in A.D. 391 on abolition of blood sacrifice.

[190]In April of 397 the emperors addressed the people on the subject of squatting in the Campus Martius by setting up shacks and shanties and in October of the following year addressed the urban prefect against the rearing of private structures that impeded traffic in the squares (*plateae*) and colonnades as well as attaching them to public or private defense walls (*moenia*, not *muri*); see *Cod. Theod.* 14.14.1 and 15.1.39 (= *Cod. Iust.* 8.11.14). These passages attest a tendency somewhat earlier than any conjectural date for the forum of Sibidius Spedius.

[191]See above, sect. II.4.

[192]See above, n. 189.

statim ut adveneret vinum.[193] In the first case the "porters who usually haul from the Storks to the Temple" (of the Sun) presumably carried the wine from a quay; in the second case, "the tax account examiners at the Storks "were to be paid as soon as the wine arrives."[194] *Ciconiae* appears to have been one place, and separate from Nixae.

Much ink has been spilled over the nature and location of the Storks.[195] In accordance with two older views that Ciconiae Nixae was a single entry in the gazetteers and that it was a dock or quay at Piazza Nicosia, Castagnoli virtually made the Trigarium and the Ciconiae Nixae a part of the Campus Martius in its narrower confines even though the Campus Martius was distinct from the others if the regionary report of Region IX has any reason.[196] Today the quay at Piazza Nicosia seems to have vanished and Castagnoli is content to refer to the hypothesis of Rougé.[197] Rougé has developed an earlier notion by which storks are likened to cranes and turned into derricks. In this vein the *ciconiae* served the river port to unload ships.[198] Moreover he cites in support of his theory a passage in Isidore on garden tools and machines that entirely disproves his theory. The bishop of Seville writes of the 'shadouf', as we call this machine that is employed to lift water—a machine normally called a *telo*, but sometimes a 'weasel' (*mustela*) or by Spaniards a stork (*ciconia*).[199] Twice, the proper definition is entered in the bilingual glosses: *ciconia* πελαργος μηχανη; κηλωνιονφριοτος *ciconia telleno*.[200] Indeed, in Latin a derrick could be called a 'crane' (*grus*).[201] What Isidore

---

[193]*CIL* VI 1785 = 31931. The date is much later than that of the foundation of the 'templum' of the Sun where the *vina fiscalia* were stored. I so stress because La Rocca, (above, n. 49), 60-65, thinks the inscription as old as the temple, i.e. 274/275. The late antique inscription recording the scale of wages and twice mentioning the Storks was found on the site of the complex of the temple of the Sun (see *CAR* II-G 90. p. 170) that is identified in part by the several dedications to the Sun, texts tinged heavily with Mithraism (see *CAR* II-G, 89, p. 169, and 93, p. 171, and 140, p. 179; *CIL* VI 749-754; *ILS* 4267-4269). As the crow flies the shortest distance from the temple complex at the Via Flaminia (at the site of long dismantled Arco di Portogallo) to the Tiber (Lungotevere Marzio) is ca. 450 m. See Plan 1.

[194]See A. H. M. Jones, *The Later Roman Empire* 2 vols. (Norman 1964), 704-705, 1291; cf. Chastognol (above, n. 163), 326-330. Flambard (above, n. 109) makes the *professionarii* 'personnel'; he, too, dates this inscription to the late third century.

[195]See, e.g., La Rocca, loc. cit., above, n. 193, who naturally wants to situate it according to his theories.

[196]Castagnoli (above, 12) pp. 140-148.

[197]F. Castagnoli, "Installazione portuali a Roma," *MAAR* 36 (1980), p. 35; La Rocca (above n. 49), 61.

[198]J. Rougé, "Ad Ciconias Nixas," *Rev. Et. Anc.* 59 (1957) pp. 320-328; idem, *Recherches sur l'organisation du commerce maritime en Méditerranée dans l'empire romain* (Paris 1966), 163-165, who does not know the real function of the *professionarii* (see Jones, above, n. 194).

[199]Isid. *Etym.* 20.15 in the chapter *de instrumentis hortorum*. *Ciconia* was also the name of a tool to measure the size of a trench (Columella 3.13.11).

[200]*Corp. Gloss. Lat.* 2.100, 349. A *kelon* was a swing beam for drawing water.

[201]Vitr. *Arch.* 10.13.3. A mechanical crane is carved on the Haterii relief (Vatican inv. no. 9998). There is none on the relief of the Ostian port. See Meiggs (above, n. 50), pl. XX.

describes is a "water-driven, water-lifting wheel with compartmental rim," i.e. a shadouf.[202] It is true that in the unique document of the Ciconiae 'drawers' (*haustores*) are paid and that some such devices draw water. However the *haustores* of the inscription of wages are not associated with the *ciconiae* in the sense that they operated them. Moreover, the *ciconiae* would not be needed in the activities since the wine arrived in flasks (*ampullae*) and were transferred to casks (*cupae*).[203] Only the Spaniards used the word *ciconia* for a lifting device and that lifting device was a shadouf. A *ciconia* was not a crane or a derrick. A shadouf was not needed on the banks of the Tiber river. Another explanation of the storks must be sought even if it merely recalls some monument decorated with these birds.

The lack of an early notice about the Ciconiae may be owed to its foundation by the emperor Aurelian. To him is securely attributed the introduction of a new Sun god into a newly founded Roman temple in whose colonnades were installed the administration and distribution of the *vina fiscalia*. Moreover he arranged for the several bureaux to handle the state promotion of its own wine trade: *ratio dogae, cuparum navium et operum*.[204] The evidence for Aurelian's reinforcement of the Tiber banks remains slim. In a letter to a prefect of the city's food supply, very likely the author's invention, Aurelian is made to write: "navicularios Niliacos apud Aegyptum novos et Romae amnicos posui, Tiberinas extruxi ripas, vadum alvei tumentis effodi, diis et Perennitati vota constitui. . . ."[205] The palpably non-existent goddess Perennitas permits an attempt at establishing the truth of the facts but not of the letter. Perennitas ought to be construed as the old goddess Anna Perenna whose annual festival on 15 March was observed at the first milestone on the Via Flaminia by the Tiber River.[206] One of the false etymologies of her name Anna was based on the word for riverstream *amnis*.[207] In the purported letter of Aurelian *Perennitas* follows upon mention of the rivershippers at Rome, river-bed dredging and river bank reinforcement. Probably the Latin text should read *Perennae*. In the last liturgical calendar derived from Roman paganism, that of Filocalus at mid-fourth century, the feast of Anna Perenna has dropped from 15 March but at

---

[202]J. P. Oleson, *Greek and Roman Mechanical Water-lifting Devices: The History of a Technology* (Toronto 1984), 56–57, 179, 325–350.

[203]*CIL* VI 1785 = 31931; Oleson (last note), pp. 41–42, 46–48, 113–114; 396–397. For representations of taking wine off ships see Meiggs (above, n. 50), pl. XXVI and R. E. A. Palmer, "The Topography and Social History of Rome's Trastevere (Southern Sector)," *Proc. Amer. Philos. Soc.* 125 (1981): 394.

[204]*HA Aurelian* 31.7, 35.3, 39.2, 6; 48. Aurelius Victor (*Caes.* 35.7) and the *Chronicler of the year 354* second only the *Historia Augusta's* report of the state assumption of free dole of meat, salt, and olive oil. See Palmer (above, n. 175), 220. For the temple's closeness to the Tiber see above, n. 193.

[205]*HA Aurelian* 47.3 The river's reinforced embankments still stood in the year 554; see Ward-Perkins (above, n. 163), 47.

[206]See Degrassi (above, n. 2), 423–424.

[207]Ovid *Fast.* 3.651–654.

18 June there is fixed an entirely unknown feast of Anna.[208] I propose that this Anna Perenna is the foundation of Aurelian.[209] If the establishment of new rites for Anna Perenna is affirmed by the emendation of the text and interpretation of the subsequent calendar, then we may assume that the Tiber banks, at least by the foot of the Aurelianic wall were indeed reinforced. At that time Ciconiae itself may have been established as a station for the wine.

Still the quay or dock where the wine as tax payment in kind reached Rome bore the name of the Storks for reasons unknown. In the next section the location of the quarter or street of the Storks, whatever the name meant, can be fixed approximately, once and for all.[210]

II.10 St. Tryphon's

The church of St. Augustine, which has figured in the account of the dedication to Silvanus Pantheus, of the inscription of Socrates' prayer to Pan, and to the large vaulted building earlier identified tentatively as the Athenaeum, succeeded to the property of an early church of St. Tryphon whose foundation date is unknown.

St. Tryphon's is mentioned in the *ordo* of the Canon Benedict, perhaps compiling in the middle of the tenth century: *proficiscens ad sanctam Mariam in Aquiro, ad arcum Pietatis, sic ascendit ad Campum Martium transiens ante Sanctum Trifonem iuxta posterulas usque ad pontem Hadrianum.*[211] The church was rebuilt in 1006 by the Fountain of the Sow and in 1287 was assigned to the Augustinians who dedicated their first church to Augustine in 1358.[212] (See Plan 2, nos. 5 and 9.)

The posterns mentioned as landmarks by Benedict were set in Aurelian's wall. In the Middle Ages one was named for the church of S. Lucia della Tinta and another for a pillar in ruins on the Tiber em-

---

[208]Degrassi (above, n. 2), 472.

[209]Aurelian's feast of the Sun on 25 December (later Natalis Christi) stands in this calendar of Filocalus; see Degrassi (above, n. 2), 545.

[210]Flambard (above, n. 109), 204-210 makes a strong case for identifying the stork with the notion of Pietas and, specifically, for identifying these storks with an altar to Pietas raised on the occasion of the divinization of Hadrian's wife Sabina. This altar he would place in sight of Hadrian's Mausoleum. If the birds of the monument Ciconiae stand for Pietas, as well they might, I would situate them as I do in the next section.

[211]R. Valentini and G. Zucchetti, *Codice topografico della Città di Roma* vol. 3 = *Fonti per la Storia d'Italia* 90 (Rome 1946), 218; see Castagnoli (above, n. 12), 142.

[212]Valentini and Zucchetti, ibid.; and in vol. 4, pp. 95-96. They mark the disappearance of the church of St. Tryphon ca. 1750, whereas R. Lanciani, *Storia degli Scavi* (above, n. 10) 2.67 offers testimony that it was demolished ca. 1537 to make way for a new refectory. Lanciani also supplies here early evidence that some of the installations in St. Tryphon's were transported to the already existent St. Augustine's. Lanciani plots it on *Forma Vrbis Romae*, pl. 15, fronting on the Via della Scrofa. The former convent of the Augustinians today houses the Avvocatura dello Stato. At Via della Scrofa, 84, is immured the still surviving relief of the sow which named the street in the Middle Ages.

bankment.[213] In the immediate proximity of St. Lucia's appeared the tablet of the August altar ordered by Jupiter in A.D. 1 and in the church itself the altar discussed above in sect. II.3.

Who was St. Tryphon? He was martyred by Decius, or so legend has it. No sign of interest in this Phrygian saint is found in Rome in the documents of the early growth of the Roman church.[214] It is quite likely that Tryphon's worship migrated west in the wake of his popularity as a wonder-worker in the east. The onset of Tryphon's eminence can be approximately dated in the reign of Justinian. Procopius numbers the church of St. Tryphon built on the Street of the Stork in Constantinople[215] among the churches and shrines that that emperor built.

When a church was later built for him at Rome under direct or indirect Byzantine influence the founder chose, I am sure, to set it down at the Ciconiae, the Storks. In other words, the very vicinity some topographers had divined for the Storks entirely without knowledge of Justinian's foundation at his eastern capital proves as accurate a guess as could be made in circumstances falling short of a clear indication on Roman soil. I firmly believe that no one should gainsay the Byzantine influence.

Tryphon's church at Rome was by the Fountain of the Sow. In the ceremonies of the Secular Games Augustus and Septimius Severus prayed at night by the Tiber, "Mother Earth, may sacrifice be done you with the pregnant sow to be wholly consumed, I beg you, and I pray that you increase the empire and the greatness of the Roman people at war and at home and that the Latin people remain subject for ever."[216]

---

[213]I. A. Richmond, *The City Wall of Imperial Rome* (Oxford 1930), 236-238. The exact location of the posterns in question cannot be ascertained from available evidence. The church of St. Lucia, called after dyers, was early called "Sancta Lucia Quattuor Portarum" by the same Benedict Canonicus, mentioned above (n. 211), 286. See Plan 2, no. 4.

[214]His feast day, along with that of fellow martyr Respicius and the adventitious Nympha of Palermo, stood in the Roman liturgy at 10 November until displaced by Andrew Avellino. The "martyrology" of Tryphon is a western confection of bits and pieces from disparate hagiography. See A. Amore, *Bibliotheca Sanctorum* 2 (1969): 656-657. The oldest attestation of St. Tryphon in the west is derived from the inscription of a reliquary associated with the Milanese Sts. Gervasius and Prostasius at African Sufetula and dated to ca. 600. His martyr cult in Africa followed the Byzantine reconquest. For both this African evidence and a review of other notices of his cult in the western Mediterranean (Dalmatia, and in Italy, Capua, and Naples) see Yvette Duval, Loca sanctorum Africae: *Le culte des martyres en Afrique du IVᵉ au VIIᵉ siècle* = Collection de l'Ecole Française de Rome 58 (Paris, 1982) vol. 1, pp. 81-83, vol. 2, pp. 655, 667-668, and "Les saints vénérés dans l'Eglise byzantine d'Afrique," *Corsi di cultura sull'arte ravennate e bizantina* 30 (1983): 132.

[215]Proc. *Aed.* 1.9.15: καὶ Τρύφωνι δὲ ἀνέθηκεν ἱερὸν μάρτυρι, πόνῳ τε καὶ χρόνῳ πολλῷ ἐς κάλλος ἀποτετορνευμένον ἀμύθητον ὅλως, ἐν τῇ τῆς πόλεως ἀγυιᾷ τοῦ Πελαργοῦ ἐπώνυμός ἐστιν.

Procopius's admiration need not be taken seriously. S. Ferri, "Ciconiae Nixae" *Pont. Accad. Rom. Arch. Rend.* 27 (1952-54): 29-32, while writing about what are now considered two places as if one, cites evidence for a monument adorned with storks situated in Constantinople. Flambard (above, n. 109), 193-194 discusses other evidence on the Constantinopolitan "storks."

[216]The *acta* of Augustus, lines 134-137; of the Severi, Va 49-51. The Latin of the victim is *sus plena prodigiva*. See Pighi (above, n. 23), 116-117, 162-163, 303. On the absence of

The Fountain of the Sow may or may not reflect that sacrifice made every one hundred or one hundred and ten years. If doubts linger in this regard, they cannot, I believe, linger in the matter of a present day phenomenon within the church of St. Augustine.

That the Nixae, a monument of this sector, represented the women in adoration of Juno Regina of the Capital on bended knee, (*genibus nixae*)[217] or, as La Rocca would have it,[218] the Ilithyiae as goddesses of childbirth, seems most likely. What is more, the shadow of the *Nixae* hangs over St. Augustine's. For hours I have sat facing the inside of the central portal of this church which is always sealed to accommodate the hundreds of exvotos for the statue of the seated Madonna del (Divin) Parto and I have watched by candlelight scores of Roman women touch certain parts of that Christian idol in a given order.[219] Who can say whether St. Tryphon's had housed a similar Mother of God and whether she traced her pedigree to Mother Earth or the Isis with the Infant Harpocrates?

The modern Via della Scrofa runs above an ancient pavement. It must have been the Street of the Storks. The landmark naming it seems also to have named the quarter after itself. As it runs north, however, this street, whether today called Via della Scrofa or Ripetta ('Little bank'), passes by the Tiber where the *vina fiscalia* may have been unloaded. The street where the ancient Street of the Storks began will be discussed in the next section. (See both Plans 1 and 2.)

Aurelian may be held responsible for the monument(s) or like objects that gave name to the street of the Storks which cannot be attested before the middle of the fourth century. The Storks should be associated with the riverine site of the quay for offloading wine of the fisc from ships. As a name of the street Storks suggested the site of the church of St. Tryphon in conscious recollection of the site of his church built by Justinian in Constantinople.

---

the goddess Terra Mater in the dedication of the August altar in A.D. 1 and a probable substitution of Ops, see above pp. 22, 26.

[217]The *acta* of Augustus, lines 125-126; of Severus, IV 12; Pighi (above, n. 23), 116, 157.

[218]See above, at n. 193.

[219]Of course, the statue by Sansovino was carved for this fifteenth-century church. An early Christian perpetuation of the local pagan practices of promoting human fecundity may be inferred from the usage *in Lucinis* first attested in the later fourth century to denominate the quarter of the church of St. Lawrence (see *Epistulae imperatorum pontificum . . . Avellana . . . Collectio* 1.5) as *in Lucinis* or *Lucina*. Apparently opposite this sector was the *Pariturium*, solely noted by the Einsiedeln pilgrim (*ca.* 800). Attempts have been made to link this entirely obscure "birthing" to Juno Lucina; see R. Valentino and G. Zucchetti, *Codice topografico della città di Roma* 2 (1942) 186. The only attestation of Juno Lucina in this part of Rome is that that I have restored to *CIL* VI 30975, above sect. II.3, at nn. 39 and 40. Too many links, if links there were, are missing in a chain of evidence down to the Madonna del Parto. Flambard (above, n. 109) reaches the conclusion that the late antique toponym *in Lucinis* must refer to Juno Lucina or, more exactly, plural Lucinae who were the Nixae. But the church of S. Lorenzo in Lucina stands far distant from the site of Tarentum where the Ilithyiae were worshipped.

II.11 The Covered Way

In his satire on the apotheosis of the emperor Claudius Seneca represents the departure from Rome: "The Talthybius of the gods lays claim to him and drags him away with his head muffled so that none can recognize him, and descends to the Underworld between the Tiber and the Covered Way."[220] A generation later Martial also mentioned the Covered Way (*Via Tecta*). Sending his latest book from Imola in northern Italy to his friend Julius Martialis, he directs that it go at once to the beginning of the Covered Way where Julius lives in a house formerly belonging to Daphnis.[221] Given the itinerary, the book would have traveled to the city by the Via Flaminia. The third and last reference to the Covered Way, also from Martial, links it to the Via Flaminia. A Lingonian Gaul is going home late at night and has gone down the Covered and Flaminian Ways, stubs his toe and stumbles. His frail slave cannot heave the hulk to his feet and so hails four slaves carrying a bier to a pauper's pyre. They dump their cheap load and take up the sprawling Lingonian.[222] The bier-porters are doubtless going outward (i.e. north) on the Flaminian Way where the cremation and burial would take place.[223] The statement of this epigram squares with the inference from the earlier epigram that the Covered Way intersected or joined the Flaminian Way.

The Senecan passage has long been considered to refer to the Tarentum as the place where Claudius, led by Mercury, descended to the Underworld.[224] The longstanding view that Via Tecta was a NS street, later called in part Porticus Maximae,[225] cannot be sustained. That street runs more or less in the same direction as the Via Flaminia. The Lingonian Gaul could not have gone home by two distinct and somewhat parallel streets running in the same direction. Therefore the Covered Way must be sought elsewhere. If the street is to lead to the Tarentum, the choice is one.

---

[220]Sen. *Apoc.* 13.1 The divine Talthybius is Mercury as Psychopompos.

[221]Martial 3.5. Julius Martialis is *PIR*[2] J 411. The origin of the book was Forum Cornelii (Martial 3.4).

[222]Mart. 8.75.

[223]Martial (6.28) and Statius (*Silv.* 2.1.175ff.) write of the tomb of the same freedman on the Via Flaminia. Cf. Martial 11.13. Another burial along that road is mentioned by Juvenal (*Sat.* 1.170) whose scholiast says the road had the tombs of the nobility. There is partial confirmation of the scholium; see *CAR* II-A 15, p. 13; 27, p. 15; 34, p. 17.

[224]See Chr. Huelsen, *Topographie der Stadt Rom im Altherthum* 1.3 (Berlin 1907), 485 and 503.

[225]Ibid. 485; Platner-Ashby, *TDAR*, p. 568; Castagnoli (above, n. 12) p. 156; La Rocca (above, n. 49) pp. 66-69. Of course this identification was born of the belief that remains under the Piazza Sforza-Cesarini had been correctly identified by Lanciani as the Tarentum; see his *Forma Vrbis Romae*, pl. 14. The Porticus Maximae are thought to have flanked the approach to Hadrian's Bridge which did not exist when Seneca and Martial wrote.

Beneath the Piazza Colonna on the Corso (= Via Flaminia), the Via
delle Copelle, Via di S. Agostino, and Via dei Coronari lies a straight
way that led directly to the Tarentum.[226] This EW street is the only
choice for identification as the Covered Way since alone it meets the
indications of Seneca and Martial who did not know how to cross Hadrian's bridge.[227] (See both Plans 1 and 2.)

Coming from the center of the city Romans in the first century A.D.
would have gone north by the Flaminian Way and turned west onto the
Covered Way. The first junction would have come at the street later
called Street of the Storks, now the Via della Scrofa intersecting the
Via di S. Agostino. The second junction would have come at the street
that later passed by the new forum of Sibidius Spedius, now the Via dei
Soldati. The latter street would have reached a dead end at Aurelian's
wall after the 270s unless there was an ancient postern let in the wall
here by the later site of the church of St. Lucia. The last junction would
have come at the street, now the Via del Banco di S. Spirito, but only
that portion running south since its northern tract presumably could
not have run north to the Pons Aelius until the next century. Finally the
street would have ended at the *platea* of the Tarentum.[228] This long
street is a stretch of pavement extending almost 1.5 km. That it was
"covered" from end to end seems doubtful. In truth we are speaking of a
street flanked on one or both sides by colonnade.

However we are well advised to bear in mind that the Covered Way is
mentioned only in the latter half of the first century A.D. and might
have had other names. Moreover, its beginning at the Via Flaminia
would have been much modified by the Antonine monuments (e.g. the
Column of M. Aurelius) reared in the next century. (See Plan 1.)

Provision for temporary shelter from the elements was doubtless the
motive in building a colonnade along the route. Just as Pompey the
Great built a quadrangular colonnade beside his theater to accommodate theater goers, the builder of the Covered Way took into account
those attending festivals in this zone. If the colonnade ran north of the
street and if it was raised, it could have served as a mole (island?) and
breakwater when the river flowed over its banks.[229]

---

[226]Traces of this street have long been known and are now charted on *CAR* I, grid
squares H and I and *CAR* II, grid square G. I am aware that when the MS of Seneca was
thought to read Via Recta (sic) this ancient street was given that name; see Lanciani,
FVR, pl. 14, Huelsen (above, n. 224), 503.

[227]Willfully blinkered, students of the problem have ignored Martial's directions to his
book and the route for his Lingonian Gaul.

[228]See Quilici Gigli (above, n. 109).

[229]From the evidence of a newly discovered fragment of a plan of ancient Rome it is
clear that along the left bank of the Tiber near the Island and where today lies the Ghetto
were not only commercial houses serving the port but also a porticated street which as F.
Castagnoli, "Un nuovo documento per la topografia di Roma antica", *Studi Romani* 33
(1985) pp. 205-211 states, was the *ripa*. If such was the development and use of land
downstream, a *via tecta* will have served a like purpose upstream.

II.12 Conclusions

When Augustus and his son-in-law Agrippa turned to the urbanization of the Campus Martius in its broadest sense, they were following in
the path of Pompey whose great theatrical complex was completed in
the year 54 B.C. when the censors were for the first time subjecting the
river banks to a thorough reinforcement of a kind that was repeated in
succeeding generations. Flood control remained a problem but one of
less severity and frequency for the next centuries.

At the northern end where the Tiber turned twice in its course two
disparate religious modes had been observed in the preceding centuries.
The cult of Mars thrice yearly required chariot races and sacrifice. In
marked contrast, every century at the Tarentum serial rites were held
for divinities whose very names testified to their thoroughly Hellenic
origins. These rites, extended to include divinities on the Capitol and,
in Augustus's reign, the Palatine, included stageplays and chariot races.
Some of these religiously inspired entertainments were presented in the
immediate vicinity of the Tarentum which, so far as we know, meant
only the place where the altar of Dis and Proserpina was buried in the
long interval of a *saeculum*.

The early appearance of Isis and her child Harpocrates in the quarter
surprises less if we remember their close relation to the Nile River that
might be replicated here by the river of Rome with its waterborne traffic. Whether Mars or the Ilithyiae or Isis, the gods promoted fertility of
the land and its people. Such a religious function can be traced, albeit
by a broken line, down to the peculiar efficacy of the Madonna del
Parto now in the church of St. Augustine.

In imitation of the great traditional games for Jupiter Optimus Maximus held every September, the senate decreed that the consul give votive games for the return of Augustus. In 13 and 7 B.C. these games
were performed in the region. Since the same kind of *ludi votivi* were
given in 8 B.C. on the Campus Martialis of the Caelian Hill, it has been
argued that the games dedicated to Jupiter Best and Greatest followed
the practice of the chariot races for Mars in time of flood or no.

A portion of the votive games were stageplays which were memorial-
ized by the theatrical masks of marble found with records of the games
of 13 B.C. and 7 B.C. To the same sector I have assigned Augustus's gift
of a statue of Jupiter the Tragic Player to what was a newly founded
compitum, a crossroads shrine of the neighborhood.

Jupiter's cult here was further observed shortly before A.D. 1 when
the god himself bade the rearing of an August altar to a group of gods.
The choice of these gods reflects the enduring influence of Augustus
and Agrippa's Secular Games in 17 B.C. as well as the new presence of
the divine queen of the Nile.

Given the quarter's openness to strange gods, the subsequent arrival
of the cult of a universal god seems meet. In the second century came
Silvanus Pantheus, otherwise attested in the role of a deity of good
health. His epithet betokened a universality unknown to Rome in
former times. In the third century came Pan whose very name betokened universality and whose physical attributes, the heavenly bodies.
So closely linked with Silvanus, Pan represented the sum of natural
matter, ὕλη that was *silva* in Latin. These gods might seem lowly re-
flexes of lowly men. Pan, however, was here represented to the Romans
by the device of inscribing Plato's Socratic prayer to Pan, a Pan who
had the reputation of rhetorical invention.

The first emperor and a senate devoted to his well-being promoted
the building development of the sector. One or, more likely, two permanent stages were reared for some of the Secular play-giving in the first
place and in the second place for the play-giving of the votive games for
Augustus's return. Such stages would have been decorated with monumental theatrical masks. Here, too, Jupiter the Tragic Player would
have received the worship of the residents of a new neighborhood
whose *magistri* were launched on the perpetuation of the innovative cult
of the Lares Augusti. One of their kind was literally inspired by Jupiter
to foster the cult of many gods.

Consuls and princes gave their games here in association with the
annual and the centennial religious ceremonies. It has long been held
that the chariot races required by cult were run on the tract called the
Trigarium which I have argued lay in this sector.

Beside the benefactions of structures intended for occasional and rare
entertainments rose, it has been proposed, the Athenaeum. This was
Hadrian's school of the liberal arts and long survived the emperors'
removal to other imperial capitals. Its theater-like hall attracted boister-
ous crowds to hear rhetorical and philosophical performances. In the
shadow of its influence a public speaker from Byzantium was appropri-
ately acknowledged for his good governance. Further, the same atmo-
sphere may have prompted this choice of place, whatever exactly it was,
for the inscription of the prayer to Pan. The quotation from the *Phaedrus* had been rendered in a manner to suggest conscious linguistic ne-
glect. I have proposed that its rendition is of a piece with Porphyry's
account of his teacher Plotinus's habits.

Between the inscription of Socrates's prayer in the latter half of the
third century and of the decoration of a new forum in the early fifth
century no telltale epigraphic evidence informs us on this sector. After
the restraints were applied to pagan rites, a nobleman of illustrious
lineage founded a forum where his son reared togate statues of the
founder, of his father-in-law, and of a distant maternal ancestor.

This new forum may have occupied what remained of the Trigarium
or other sites dedicated to the observance of religious ceremonies

grown obsolete. Earlier encroachment on the terrain of this horse-exercising ground is known from the tombstone of a man who had a lead plant there. The destination of his lead products is not known. Equally uncertain are the articles traded in the new forum of Sibidius Spedius.

Although some activity in trade must have occurred in this sector since the days of Augustus, we are not in a position to identify the articles of trade until the establishment of a quay for receipt of the *vina fiscalia* borne by river boats. The state wine traffic was plied between this quay at the Storks and the Temple of the Sun on the Flaminian Way where a warehouse was maintained in its adjacent colonnade.

Under a much later Byzantine influence a church to St. Tryphon was founded on what is today the Via della Scrofa, named after an ancient fountain decorated with the small relief of a sow. Since his famous church in Constantinople was built by Justinian on the Street of the Stork, the ancient name of the street chosen for his Roman church can be identified as Storks (*Ciconiae*), a name probably given to the quarter as well as to the continuation (today the Ripetta) of the Via della Scrofa.

The arterial road of this sector ran west from the Via Flaminia and was called the Covered Way (*Via Tecta*). Its beginning will have undergone considerable modification under the Antonines to make way for new monuments.

As the Via Tecta proceeded west after the Street of the Storks it passed the Nixae at the Via degli Acquasparta where the October Horse was sacrificed and apparently ended its course at the Tarentum until Hadrian's reign when one could turn north and cross the river by the bridge to his Mausoleum.

INDEX

9 780871 698025